WORSHIP WALK

Where Worship and Life Intersect

D1413724

makeusholy *publishing*

WORSHIP WALK

Where Worship and Life Intersect

Gareth J. Goossen

Love GOD, your God,

walk in all his ways,

do what he's commanded,

embrace him, serve him

with everything you are and have.

Joshua 22:5b (The Message)

Worship Walk
Where Worship and Life Intersect

All Scripture quotations, unless otherwise noted, are taken from the HOLY BIBLE, NEW INTERNATIONAL VERSION®. NIV®. Copyright© 1973, 1978, 1984 by International Bible Society. Used with permission of Zondervan Publishing House.

The testimonies herein are true. Some names and non-essential details have been changed for the sake of confidentiality.

All italics herein were added by the author for emphasis, unless otherwise stated.

Cover design and photography by Heather Lee at Barefoot Creative, Inc. Interior design and layout by Dan Snyder at Barefoot Creative, Inc.

Library and Archives Canada Cataloguing in Publication

Goossen, Gareth J., 1955-
　　　　Worship walk : where worship and life intersect / Gareth J. Goossen.

Includes bibliographical references.
ISBN 0-9736900-0-3

　　　　1. Worship.　I. Title.

BV10.3.G68 2004　　　　248.3　　　　C2004-906691-9

makeusholy *publishing*
Kitchener, Ontario, Canada

www.makeusholy.org
worshipwalk@makeusholy.org

*This book is dedicated to my wife Gayle
and our three children; Chris, Dan and Carine.*

Paul was all ready to speak,
but before he could utter a word Gallio said . . .
Acts 18:14a (Phillips)

FOREWORDS

Things other people say about the book . . .

FOREWORD BY BRIAN DOERKSEN

At the very heart of worship is our longing to know and love God! *Worship Walk* helps bring us back to that heart in a compelling way!

I have spent most of my life asking along with the psalmist – "when can I go and meet with God" (Psalm 42:2)? I believe this is the cry of our hearts because a genuine meeting with him is the only thing that really satisfies. Yet I am amazed at how often we, as worship leaders, seem to think that our job at our weekly gatherings is to excite or entertain God's people! We need fresh reminders that the main reason people have gathered is a hunger to meet with God. And that meeting with God can be facilitated by more than just music! Gareth has it right when he says people are not mainly coming to church to be entertained (there are better places for that!) but to find God.

Is that what we are offering in our churches? An encounter with the living God? Is that what we are expecting to experience during the rest of our week?

We were created for fellowship with our Creator and it's only that ongoing encounter that truly renews us! In our lives, when we get tired and overwhelmed, we often turn to entertainment and we are distracted for a time . . . but not deeply satisfied. But the presence of God that we encounter in genuine worship will satisfy. So this is the goal of each worship gathering; that we would encounter God! And this is the goal of our daily walk with God – that we would encounter God along the journey!

There are many powerful truths covered in this book – I love the way Gareth helps us to remember the truth of the cost of worship. God is more committed to forming his character in us than he is in providing for our comfort. And so worship involves aspects of our whole life. The chapters on confession and silence are fantastic and critical for us to understand how worship is walked out in our lives.

This book is a timely reminder of what worship is all about and how we are to walk it out in our lives.

— *Brian Doerksen*

BRIAN DOERKSEN

Brian Doerksen has always had a passion for intimate worship. Son of Harry and Agnes Doerksen, he was raised in a Christian home in Abbotsford, British Columbia, and was a member at a local Mennonite Brethren church, graduating from Mennonite Educational Institute in 1983. In 1984, at 19 years old, he married his high school sweetheart Joyce and they began married life serving with Youth with a Mission in Southeast Asia. As a 22-year-old, he was asked to join the staff of the Langley Vineyard Christian Fellowship and spent several years there as the worship pastor in the late 80s and early 90s. Some of his first published songs from that period were **Faithful One**, **Refiner's Fire** *and* **I Lift My Eyes Up.**

He lived in London, England, from 1997–1999, where he trained worship leaders and songwriters in the UK and Ireland and produced **Hungry** *(Best Worship Project 2001 Praise Awards – "Worship Leader Magazine"). After returning to Canada, he produced two worship albums for Vineyard Music:* **Believe** *(2000) and* **All I Need** *(2001).*

In 2002, he produced the first album of his worship songs called **You Shine.** *It was recorded live in Dublin, Ireland, and it was released in September 2002 in over 170 nations by Integrity. His songs include* **Come, Now is the Time to Worship,** *currently one of the fastest climbing songs on the CCLI charts,* **Light the Fire Again, Hallelujah (Your Love is Amazing)** *– a co-write with Brenton Brown,* **More, You Shine** *and* **Hope of the Nations.** *He is also developing a musical of hope for the fatherless called* **Father's House.**

His second album of his worship songs was released in 2004 called **Today.** *Recorded live in his home town of Abbotsford, BC, Canada, it contains 15 songs including:* **Everlasting, The River, Refiner's Fire, Creation Calls** *and* **Lead Us Lord.**

He and his family, wife of 17 years Joyce and six children Rachel, Esther, Benjamin, Joy, Mercy and Isaiah, live in Abbotsford, British Columbia, Canada, in the expanding old farmhouse he was raised in since childhood.

Website: http://www.briandoerksen.com

WORSHIP WALK

FOREWORD BY DR. PETER H. DAVIDS

In 1993, Brian Doerksen sent me an invitation to be the speaker at a conference in Kitchener, Ontario. He was to be the worship leader. That *Make Us Holy: Worship and Renewal Conference* had been organized by Gareth Goossen, whom I met upon my arrival. I was immediately impressed by his desire for worship to engage all of our lives, not just our times of singing to God, and as a result I have followed his ministry – first in the local church and then in his founding *Make Us Holy* as a vehicle to take his burden to the wider church – ever since.

When I teach Biblical Expressions of Worship, I have almost nothing to say about music (which has not survived), although I do have more to say about the lyrics (e.g. the Psalms or the songs found in Revelation). The core of worship is found in the terminology, which in both Hebrew and Greek means 'to bow before' – in the sense of submitting to, giving honour to – someone, 'to be in awe of' someone, or 'to render service to' someone. In other words, Christianity is, for us who have come to pledge our allegiance to Jesus, the true Islam (the term 'Islam' means 'submission'). That core attitude works itself out in our service and our singing, and our service in the world is just as much worship as our singing in the gathered congregation. Worship is seen in our praise of God in nature and our care for the environment because our Master made it. It is seen in our engagement for social justice in our country and community, in how we live in our household (living with the sense that Jesus is present there at all times and thus our treatment of our spouses and children is a service and submission to him), and in what we do when gathered with other believers, i.e. 'in church'. That is the message of this book. Gareth has caught the vision and has done a good job of communicating it in a practical and down-to-earth way. Unlike me, he resists any temptation to put you to sleep with discussions of Hebrew and Greek, but instead wakes you up with lively contemporary stories.

Worship depends upon our relationship with Jesus and his Father. Richard Foster includes it as one of the spiritual disciplines. Dallas Willard comments upon it in the same context. Gareth subsumes spiritual disciplines, such as silence, under the topic of worship. This is indeed an appropriate insight. Spirituality is a new catchword of our age, and it certainly should be. Too long our churches have been too happy with outward forms rather than inward reality. But, as Dallas Willard argues (The Spirit of the Disciplines), spiritual discipline serves a greater purpose. Gareth Goossen shows us this greater purpose – it is worship, the giving of ourselves to our Master. And it begins in a heart that is quiet and submitted and thus hears the voice of the Master; that works itself out in actions of service under the guidance of that voice. And that inner submission rises to a crescendo as a group of worshippers gather together and express verbally in song what they have been living day by day the rest of the week. This unity of spirituality, service and expressive worship is exquisitely caught by Gareth, and hopefully will be caught by those of you who read this book.

I recommend that you do not read this book too fast. Read it one chapter at a time and then meditate on each chapter. Let it sink into your soul. Practice living it out by means of the exercises that he suggests. If you do that, I believe that you will find your life renewed, for you will be entering into the heart of worship, which is really nothing other than entering into the heart of God.

— **Peter Davids**

Dr. Peter H. Davids

Peter H. Davids, Ph.D. and his wife, Judith L. Davids, M.C.S., have served as missionary educators in Europe, providing biblical-theological and counselling services and training to churches and Christian leaders in both the German-speaking world and the surrounding areas of Eastern and Western Europe. Now residing in Stafford (Houston) Texas, Peter continues to work as a self-employed biblical scholar and church consultant with a focus on Europe and Canada.

*Peter Davids is perhaps known especially for his scholarly treatment of **The Epistle of James: A Commentary on the Greek Text** for the New International Greek Testament Commentary series (Eerdmans Publishing). He reworked his research on the Epistle for the more pastorally based commentary **James**, Volume 15 of the New International Biblical Commentary series. He wrote **James' Message** in B. Chilton and J. Neusner, eds., **The Brother of Jesus** for Westminster John Knox Press.*

*He wrote **Spirit and Ethics: The Holy Spirit and the Use of Wealth in the New Testament** for Sheffield Academic Press and **Discipleship in the Epistle of James** for Eerdmans Publishing. He also authored the **First Epistle of Peter** for the New International Commentary on the New Testament series.*

*He has authored **More Hard Sayings of the New Testament** and co-authored **Hard Sayings of the Bible** with Walter C. Kaiser and F. F. Bruce for InterVarsity Press. He has recently co-edited the book **Dictionary of the Later New Testament & its Developments** with Ralph P. Martin, again for InterVarsity Press.*

*Peter is also a contributing writer for Zondervan Publishing's "**Illustrated Bible Backgrounds Commentary Set** for Matthew, Mark, Luke; John, Acts; Romans to Philemon; Hebrews to Revelation. He has recently contributed to Brill Academic Publishing's **The Missions of James, Peter, and Paul: Tensions in Early Christianity.***

Website: http://davidsnet.ws/biblical

TABLE OF CONTENTS

PART 1

Getting Started . . .

Happy are those who hear the joyful call to worship,
for they will walk in the light of your presence, LORD.
Psalm 89:15 – NLT

INTRODUCTION

Laying the foundation

Worship . . .

Worship changes who we are as we pursue who God is.

Music has always been a powerful medium to carry the truth of who God is and how he is calling us to worship him. Today, the church is focused so strongly on the power of music that we have begun confusing music with worship. Well-meaning, God-honouring men and women engage in bitter battles with their brothers and sisters in the Lord over the 'best' style of expressing worship in song. While they have prayer for renewal within their church, they take their eyes off God and look to music to be that which ignites renewal.

Music and worship are not synonymous. True worship changes us when God draws us into his presence. We cannot remain the same. When the image of the invisible God momentarily crosses our senses we are undone – completely decimated by the wonder of a God who gives us the privilege of an audience.

At the moment of meeting God, trivialities of earthly possessions and positions diminish in his presence. We want nothing for ourselves – only what we can give to him. Light, life and love become centred in harmony with who he is and what he desires. This is a romance which is totally focused on the object of our affection. Self is consumed within our desire to please him. Desire and passion remain unfulfilled without him receiving pleasure. Our lives are renewed and refreshed as we focus on giving God praise.

God is the almighty creator. Creation declares his praise. From the rising of the sun to its setting – all creation praises his name. God is proclaiming his presence at all times – inviting us to see him, to recognize his imprint everywhere – in everything he has made and continues to cause to exist. As the worshippers' vision changes towards God, they can recognize those imprints and extend praise to God.

Music, like God's creation, is a powerful tool to help open us up to the worship of God. Because music engages our emotions, it has the ability to draw us into a sensory experience of understanding and expressing the wonder of who God is. Our expression becomes more than intellectual assent to what we have come to know to be true, but a deeper interaction between what we know and how we have begun to experience that reality as it impacts our emotional responses to that truth.

Renewal comes from worship. True worship comes when we recognize the power and love of our God. True worship comes from our gratitude to a Saviour who, in powerful surrender, died so that we might live.

True worship comes from our hearts poised in reverent humility that understands that Jesus sent his Spirit to comfort and encourage us, to live in us as our guide, helper and friend.

Worship encompasses all of us: our emotions, our intellects, our relationships, our working lives. Our corporate expression of worship invites renewal when worshippers focus on their God – not on style, not on format, not on ritual. Our private expression of worship invites personal renewal when individuals begin to see God interacting with them in their lives, their work and their relationships.

Many times as I have walked my dog in the early morning, the wonder of God's creation has drawn me in. Seeing the snail slowly carrying his home with him as he crosses the path; discovering the bush rabbit nibbling on vegetation in the underbrush; watching a spider spin an incredible mosaic web – all these and more invite my recognition of a powerful creator God, inviting me to extend my praise to him.

It was during those walks with my dog that I began to explore the awesome ways in which God makes his presence known to his creation. God began to teach me to recognize his works, his attributes, his qualities and his characteristics – inviting my worship. As he would open up my thoughts, heart and mind to the multiplicity of ways in which he involved himself in life, my paradigm of worship began to change. I began to understand that God desired my life to be given in worship to him. He wanted me to walk with him and worship him beyond Sunday morning, beyond the music, to the whole of my life.

This book is entitled *Worship Walk: Where Worship and Life Intersect*. I believe God desires our lives to reflect an intimate, daily relationship with him. In Acts 4:13 the high priest and members of the Jewish council interviewed Peter and John after they had healed the crippled man sitting by the temple. They recognized that they had been with Jesus. The disciples had walked with Jesus daily. He not only taught them the truth of their heavenly Father, he taught them how to live from day to day as they walked along.

Jesus wants to walk with us in the whole of our lives – not just in the segment we set aside for him. As we walk with him each day and invite him to interact with us in our daily duties and tasks, he begins to draw us to a kind of worship that isn't dependent on time, place, position; that isn't dependent on music or ritual. He draws us to worship him in the journey of life – to walk with him and gain greater understanding of who he is and so reflect more of him to a world that desperately needs to see him.

He invites us to a walk of worship. And it is more than just about music.

Many people have encouraged me to write this book. It's a daunting task – especially when I see the collection of books and articles already written. Part of me sighs and agrees with King Solomon, who writes in Ecclesiastes 12:12: "But beyond this, my son, be warned: the writing of many books is endless, and excessive devotion to books is wearying to the body" (NAS).

I am writing in obedience to a call of God – a call that is, in essence, the centre of *Make Us Holy* – the ministry I began and served under since 1994. I desire that men and women, young people and children return to worship with reverence, awe, joy and enthusiasm. I desire that through prayer, discipleship and worship, Christians would influence their friends, their neighbours, their cities and nations to become worshippers of the true God. I desire that believers everywhere would be given eyes to see the glory of our God interacting with us each day, recognizing his imprint in each activity, and would extend their lives as a fragrant offering of praise to him who is holy and worthy of our praise.

I pray that this book will not only encourage your worship of God in corporate, congregational settings but even more so that you would find many opportunities to interact with God as you walk out your worship by living each and every day in his presence – noticing him, speaking with him, seeing him, loving him, living for him.

I know all the things you do.
I have seen your hard work and your patient endurance.
I know you don't tolerate evil people.
You have examined the claims of those who say they are apostles but are not.
You have discovered they are liars.
You have patiently suffered for me without quitting.
But I have this complaint against you.
You don't love me or each other as you did at first!
Look how far you have fallen from your first love!
Turn back to me again and work as you did at first. If you don't, I will come
and remove your lampstand from its place among the churches.
Revelations 2:2-5 (NLT)

CHAPTER ONE

THE ESSENCE OF WORSHIP
A focus on God

For more than sixty years the secrets and delight of Tolkien's *The Hobbit* (1937) and *Lord of the Rings* (1954/5) were a well kept secret, savoured by fantasy and literature 'geeks'. Then Hollywood took hold! Suddenly the world was alive with tiny little men with big feet on a secret mission to save their people.

Steinbeck's *East of Eden* (1952) lay dormant on library shelves for more than 50 years until Oprah put it on her booklist in June of 2003. Suddenly there was a surge in sales.

We live at a time when anything good – or sometimes not so good – is packaged, repackaged, marketed and sold. People are drawn to success. If enough people say it's good – well, then it must be good! Products, books, movies. We see it all the time in our society.

It's really no different in the church.

My heart is filled with sadness when I find that worship has also been packaged and sold with screen savers and posters. Worship, in many ways, has become a commodity.

And the most successful packaging is through Christian worship music.

Worshipping through music is not new. Musical traditions and styles may have changed, but throughout the tradition of the Jewish community and the Christian church, music has been a strong component of corporate and individual worship.

Over the past 25 years, the church has participated in a change in music styles. The change is very similar to a change that happened in the mid to late 1800s, and just like the church then, today's church struggles with change. When change begins, many good and honest people are suspicious about the 'godliness' of the change. At every moment of dynamic and powerful change throughout the history of Christianity, the church struggled and questioned.

Think of the first Christians. Ordinary men and women were convinced that a rebel in the Jewish tradition – crucified like an ordinary thief – was the Son of God. Jewish synagogue leaders were furious. They fought and killed because of that man in history.

A whole new era began.

On October 31st, 1517, a young man named Martin Luther nailed his 95 theses on the door of a Roman Catholic church in Wittenberg, Germany.

All hell broke loose! The reformers were questioning the authority of the Pope. Later, Anabaptist reformers joined the reformation, questioning the union between church and state. They questioned the practice of indulgences and suggested that people could become believers through faith alone – that the Scriptures were for everyone to hear in a language they could understand. The reformers radically challenged the thinking and worship practices of the institutional church. The fathers of the church were livid.

Today, hundreds of thousands of churches are in conflict. While much of the language of the conflict lies in changing worship styles, that is not the true centre of the conflict. The conflict is exactly the same as it was in the days of Christ and the days of the early Reformers. Church leaders who no longer focus their ministry entirely on worshipping God have lost their first love.

While that sounds simplistic, the Bible has many warnings about us leaving our first love and letting other things take its place. In Revelation, Jesus commends the church for its refusal to tolerate evil and for being patient in their suffering, but he goes on to say: "But this I have against you, you do not love me now as you did at first. Think how far you've fallen" (Revelation 2:4-5)!

How easy it is to fall away from our first love! The distractions of family, earning a living, church meetings and programs, taking care of our possessions, education . . . and the list goes on and on.

When one loses their first love, it is easy to replace it with laws, rules and rituals. How easy for us to identify the hypocrisy and arrogance in the Jewish rabbis who counted how many steps one could take on the Sabbath before it was counted as work. How easy for us to critique the priests who were more interested in padding the coffers of the church than reaching out to the people they served.

How hard for us to see the pain and agony our God is experiencing when we focus our attention on style, musical instruments and formats.

Bruce Leafblad, a professor of church music and worship at Southwestern Baptist Theological Seminary in Texas, writes:

> *In church history, no major renewal has ever come from forms and formats, and so it is today. The great need of the church today is neither to cling to the old or to create the new forms and formats. Our greatest need today is to recover the priority of God in our worship and in the whole of life. The crisis in worship today is not a crisis of form but of spirituality* (Bruce H. Leafblad, "Worship 101," *Worship Leader Magazine,* November/December 1998, p. 25).

The essence of our worship is a focus on God – to love him, to know him, to desire what he desires and participate in what he is doing. We need to rediscover a hunger for the presence of God in every aspect of our lives. This is not something that happens only on a Sunday morning. It is something that must happen in all facets of our lives. Our worship of God – our recognition of his activity among us – must be intertwined into all we do.

We are children of a living God. How wonderful when the DNA of our heavenly Father is infused into every part of our daily lives. Living a life of worship is not limited to a service or a building. We – who were made to worship him – don't cease being God's creation when we leave the sanctuary. We don't live such segregated lives with God that he participates in our lives only during those portions of time we allow him to be active. God is always active in our lives. He is intimately interested in who we are. He has carved us on the palm of his hand and he knows us completely (Isaiah 49:15-16).

He invites us into a life of worship – a life not focused on our desires and preferences but a life focused on him and his activity in the world. A life that cannot but lift his praise in the midst of drudgery, drama or ecstasy because we see beyond our own existence and recognize his activity in and through us.

I can't stand your religious meetings.
I'm fed up with your conferences and conventions.
I want nothing to do with your religion projects,
your pretentious slogans and goals.
I'm sick of your fund-raising schemes, your public relations and image making.
I've had all I can take of your noisy ego-music.
When was the last time you sang to me? Do you know what I want?
I want justice — oceans of it. I want fairness — rivers of it.
That's what I want. That's all I want.
Amos 5: 21-24 (Msg)

CHAPTER TWO

WORSHIP AND ENTERTAINMENT ARE NOT SYNONYMOUS
Worship is for God

When our focus deteriorates to style, preference and format, it is no longer worship. When we fight within our congregations because of formats, it is sin. When we critique and ostracize people for their heartfelt worship in a style that is not our preference, we are not acting as God's children.

In the past 30 years, the Christian church has experienced a vital and dramatic change. The change is not limited to specific denominations or geographic areas. Much of the change has pivoted on music. This change has the potential to revolutionize a dead and dying church . . .

But only if we refuse to submit to the wiles of our enemy.

Part of that changing landscape has come because God is renewing his people. God is drawing people to himself in greater intimacy and understanding. He has been calling his followers to worship him in spirit and in truth. He has been calling us back into a living and vital relationship with him. And as his people have responded to his call – his wooing – songs of that interaction have begun to come forth.

Young people, bored and idealistic, have reached out to God in new ways because their hearts have been touched by the heart of God. Middle-aged 'boomers' have moved towards new worship styles because with change comes a renewed sense of God, an understanding that God is doing new things in their lives.

When people experience a life-changing vitality in their relationship with God, it attracts attention. Not only do we want to hear the stories of life-changes, we want to participate in them somehow. So we read about their experience. We sing songs that have grown out of their experience. We purchase music and emulate those same songs in our churches.

These new songs are expressions of our culture, written in the language we use today and the musical style familiar to our generation. Renewal helps us to understand that church and life are one – that the words we use in our church are not just 'religious' words set apart only for Sundays. The words we use in our church should be words we use every day. When we start to separate and fragment our lives between 'church' and 'secular' we risk relegating God to a secondary place in our lives.

In the mid-eighties this 'new' worship music was dominated by a young audience. Parents and church leaders naively believed that once the young drummer and budding guitarist graduated from high school and became leaders in the church, they would again respectfully adhere to the traditions of the church, forgetting that what they clung to as 'age-old' tradition was really just a dominant style from about 80–150 years ago. Few are the places where the truly 'age-old' traditions of singing Gregorian chants, early polyphonic music, or Anglican plainsong, are still maintained. Even the early Lutheran chorales have mostly been refitted with more modern tunes (referenced from an email by Dr. Peter Davids, 14 Oct. 2004).

But the new worship music connected with young people's hearts and God met them there. The music was instrumental in bridging the gap between society and the church. It brought the passions of our everyday life into a spiritual expression and experience of God.

Because many of the new worshippers found a new experience of God through music, many of us bought into a half-truth. We saw the format as being *the* renewal. So we looked eagerly to the next worship conference, the next worship event, the next great worship CD to experience God's nearness once more. We looked forward to the next anointed worship song or gifted worship leader to lead us to that place where we could feel the sense of God's presence – because the older songs didn't seem to 'do it' like they did last year.

Sure, the music touched us and somehow opened up an ability to respond with our whole being to our loving God. But we were duped into believing that it was the music that changed us. In our wrong thinking, we began to see worship as 'music'. And we began to promote our songs as 'the worship' that would change people's hearts.

A whole new market was created. Worship CDs, worship celebrities, worship conferences, worship TV and radio. In the way North Americans do it best – worship became a lucrative capitalistic enterprise.

We need to stop right there . . .

You need to hear me correctly. I love music. I relate to music. I can truly be ushered into God's presence through music. Music is a powerful vehicle to carry our praise and adoration heavenward – but it's only one vehicle. The best vehicle for transmitting praise and adoration to God is a renewed heart. A renewed heart, a heart of passionate pursuit of God will find a way to express worship to God whatever the context, whatever the vehicle, whatever the musical style, whatever the setting.

One Sunday morning I went to the worship service longing for God to meet me. I was away from home and visiting a church I had never attended before. When the music leader began the singing, my heart sank. This was not at all what I had desired. "God," I cried out, "I want to worship you so much but I just can't with this . . . ."

Then God spoke gently and kindly, "Gareth, do you really want to worship me?"

What a question to ask! Of course, God, you know how much I want to worship you. What do you mean by that?

After a short, pregnant moment, he continued, " . . . or do you just want to sing songs you like?"

And just like that I was faced with a dilemma of my own making. Was my heart's desire really to worship God or just to sing those songs I loved to sing? Truthfully for me, singing songs I loved and easily related to did make it easier to draw close to God in a time of corporate or private worship. So it wasn't merely a question of singing songs I didn't like or had difficulty relating to, it was a question of priorities.

God continued by saying, "Because if you really want to worship me, you can! You can worship me anywhere, in any language, with any song, with anyone leading or with no song at all . . . if it is in your heart to do it."
I had fallen victim to the comfort of the worship 'tradition' I was used to. The format had become my key to worship, not God.

Worship is not about the music: it's not about the style; it's not about the format; it's not about entertainment; it's not about the language. Worship is about focusing your heart on him! It's about desiring him to receive your praise!

Slowly, and I confess, somewhat grudgingly, I began to focus on God. The music became secondary, God became my primary focus. Even though the style and presentation was not my preferred choice, that moment of corporate worship became a blessing to me and, more importantly than that, became a blessing to God.

In our pursuit of the latest worship music or worship trend we forget that worship is not about being contemporary or traditional. Worship isn't about my likes and wants. Worship isn't about the latest anointed song leader or an age-old hymn. Worship isn't about feeling good. Worship isn't about me!

Those who have been given a gift of leading God's people into worship must focus on that: guiding the worshippers into a place where they can eagerly extend their worship to God – where they can meet God with their sacrifice of praise. God is easy about music – any music. The latest style or the oldest relic really makes no difference to him. He's only really interested in one thing – the heart of the worshipper.

Worship is for God!

I believe that this is the single most important concept in grasping what worship is all about.

Ultimately, it's not about posture, lyrics, music or style. It's not about performance, inclusion, entertainment or presentation. Worship – to be truly understood as well as practiced – is solely for God. God is the starting and ending point of worship. He is the initiator. He is the conductor and he is the audience. He is the one focus.

We don't even enter into the picture except as instruments to be used in his hands to elevate his praise. Worship of God does not exist for our pleasure but for his pleasure. God desired to bring everything together, in heaven and on earth, under Jesus so that we who put our faith and hope in him would lift our praise to our glorious God (Ephesians 1:10-12). It's all about him! It's not about us.

We love him because he first loved us (1 John 4:19). We did not choose him. He chose us in Christ Jesus to be holy – to be set apart (Ephesians 1:4). We were created in his image for the praise of his glory (Isaiah 43:5-7).

It's not about us. It's all about him!

Paul Oakley, worship leader and song writer from England, wrote a song entitled *It's All About You (Jesus, Lover of My Soul)* which contains the chorus:

> *It's all about you, Jesus*
>
> *And all this is for you*
>
> *For your glory and your fame*
>
> *It's not about me*
>
> *As if you should do things my way*
>
> *You alone are God and I surrender to your ways.*
>
> 1997 Kingsway's Thankyou Music (Paul Oakley)

Worship is truly all about him – the lover of our souls. We worship him in order that he would receive glory. We worship him by bragging about his fame – by boasting about his workmanship in us and in creation. We praise him because of his greatness and power – his kindness, mercy and love.

We have no means by which to honour and glorify him except that which he gives us – our voice, our gifts and talents, our rising and retiring, our coming and going, our every breath, our lives.

This sets our focus back on the one who created us to worship him. Worship is all about him. It is not about us.

This is not to say that we don't experience anything ourselves when we worship God. Quite the contrary. God is a loving Father and he loves to make himself known to us. He loves to affirm his love for us. He loves to speak to us, to encourage us, to direct and correct us. He cheers us on when we are discouraged. He weeps with us, holding us close to his heart when we grieve. He dances with us as we celebrate his goodness and he waits patiently – quietly calling to us when we turn our backs on him in anger, withholding our worship from him.

Like a healthy marriage, when we give unselfishly to our partner we receive a response from them. But our desire to give to our spouse should not be contingent on their responding to that gift. If so, our gift of love is ultimately self-serving and our love has become conditional. Rather we should love our partner in marriage because they are the object of our affection. We are pleased to give to them regardless of whether or not there will be an appropriate response to us in return. And again, in a healthy marriage where each partner wants to build the other one up – each receives as well as gives.

God is always communicating his presence to his people. He is always responding to us. He wants us to understand his word. He wants us to know his guidance and direction. He not only responds to us when we worship, he responds to us at all times.

But we don't worship him so that we will feel his presence, or so that he will speak to us. That's starting out on the wrong foot. We worship him because he is worthy to be praised. We worship him because he is continually revealing himself to us. We worship him because there is nothing left of value that we can hold on to.

Our worship is the response of the created to the wonder of the Creator and our need to extend ourselves back to him. It's what we were created for. All created things will proclaim the reality of the Creator.

Today the worship music industry has very much created a 'need' among believers for worship which impacts 'them'. When our worship rises and falls on our feelings and our personal sense of experience alone, we have become more followers of style than followers of God – more worshippers of 'worship' than worshippers of God. We begin to need to have the music of worship impact us and we hungrily search out that which fills that need.

We have become consumers of worship music not worshippers of God, passionate pursuers of his presence. We have become connoisseurs of this worship music phenomenon – at once overwhelmingly enthusiastic about a favoured song and critical to the extreme of that which doesn't meet our high standards for 'anointed' worship.

We come by it honestly. North American culture is pleasure-based. We adulate music stars, the lives of the rich and famous. We have fallen so far into the glut of entertainment and self-indulgence that reality TV has wormed its way into people's 'real' lives. We are entertained by watching people choose spouses, go on exotic adventures and by watching married couples placed in extreme temptation – just so we can see what happens.

So when we come together as Christians, we are tempted to recreate that performance-based, hedonistic environment. We are often driven to that which best entertains us, that which makes our time well-spent. We even choose our church because the Sunday morning service is one hour of well-executed entertainment.

We test our opinions of a worship experience with each other the same way we do with secular movies and music. "Wow, that movie really sucked!" and "Wow, worship today really sucked!"

We evaluate our worship experience by the same measuring stick that we use to evaluate entertainment. "Church was boring today." or "Man, did that lead guitar ever have awesome licks!" Our critical expressions reflect an attitude that focuses back on "me". What did I get or not get out of this experience?

It's easy to see how it happens. A talented, gifted worship leader is wonderful to follow into a time of worship. And sometimes we begin to see that worship leader as being the one who "makes worship happen". So we tend to focus on their talent, gifts and abilities rather than the Spirit of God working through them and their abilities.

Matt Redman is a gifted worship leader who served in Watford, England, at a church called *Soul Survivor* in the late 1990s. Mike Pilavachi, the pastor of the church, wrestled with the temptation to make that very gift the centre of the worship. Here's his perspective:

> *Since it began, Soul Survivor has always given plenty of time over to worshipping through music. Over the years, people have poured out their hearts to God through it, and there have been plenty of examples of great things happening as a result. However, there was a season when we realized that something was 'up' with our worship.*
>
> *At first, it was difficult to put our finger on the problem. On the surface, everything was just fine: the musicians were tuning their instruments and the soundmen were getting out of bed on time. Each service*

contained a block of songs that focused on the cross and gave people the chance to get down to business with God. To make this easier, the music was (nearly) up-to-date, the chairs had disappeared and the lights were low. What better atmosphere for young people to worship God?

Yet, we seemed to have lost the spark. We seemed to be going through the motions, but I noticed that although we were singing the songs, our hearts, were far from Him. Was it Matt Redman's fault? I listened. He wasn't singing any more off notes than usual. Then one day it clicked; we had become connoisseurs of worship instead of participants of it.

In our hearts, we were giving the worship team grades on a scale from one to ten: 'Not that song again,' 'I can't hear the bass,' 'I like the way she sings better.' We had made the band the performers of worship and ourselves the audience.

We had forgotten that we are ALL the performers of worship and that God is the audience. We had forgotten that sacrifice is central to biblical worship. We are called to offer our bodies as living sacrifices – this is OUR spiritual act of worship (Romans 12:1). We are called to offer our sacrifice of praise (Hebrews 13:15).

We were challenged to ask ourselves individually, 'When I come through the door of the church, what am I bringing as my contribution to worship?' The truth came to us: worship is not a spectator sport, it is not a product molded by the taste of the consumers. It is not about what we can get out of it; it is all about God (Paul Martin, "When The Music Fades: The Eternal Truth Behind 'The Heart of Worship.'" Online Posting. *Worship Leader Workshop Magazine.* 16 Oct. 2004. <http://www.worshipleaderworkshop.com/mag-when.htm>)

The leaders of the church did a bold and extremely risky thing. They took away the music. The very thing that had become the attraction for the church was stripped away. They began to focus on words of praise directly from God. They began to bring the worshippers back to the service. They did away with the entertainment.

Out of that experience, God renewed Matt's heart and the music returned.

THE HEART OF WORSHIP

When the music fades,

All is stripped away, and I simply come

Longing just to bring

Something that's of worth

That will bless your heart

I'll bring you more than a song

For a song in itself is not what you

have required.

You search much deeper within

Through the way things appear;

You're looking into my heart.

I'm coming back to the heart of worship

And it's all about you

All about you Jesus.

I'm sorry Lord for the thing I've made it

When it's all about you,

All about you Jesus.

King of endless worth

No one could express

How much you deserve.

Though I'm weak and poor

All I have is yours, every single breath.

c/r 1997 Kingsway's Thankyou Music (Matt Redman)

When I first heard this story, I was humbled to the point of weeping! As a pastor and worship leader who had been very involved in worship teaching, training and leading for many years, I had to admit that my Sunday morning corporate worship experience had often become exactly like that – an opportunity to evaluate and critique. And when other leaders didn't make the cut that morning I often wished that I had been leading because I would have done a better job!

Can you hear the chorus, "It's all about me, Jesus. And all this is for me, for my glory and my fame . . . ?"

You see, worship and entertainment are not synonymous. Just because we have been entertained by a talented worship team, attracted by the rhythm and flow, or felt moved by the arrangement of our favourite song does not mean we have worshipped.

It's so easy to take our focus off God and put it onto the format itself. We will never be able to become true worshippers of God if we do not learn this first and ultimate principle.

Worship is for God and God alone.

No one who puts his hand to the plough and looks back
is fit for service in the kingdom.
Luke 9:62

CHAPTER THREE

THE COST OF WORSHIP
Dying to self and living for Christ

Speaking about 'cost' and 'worship' in the same sentence seems a little ironic. How could great worship – an amazing experience – come with a cost?

Serving God comes with a cost . . . a cost many of us haven't calculated to the fullest. Our theology is a little messed up here. For some reason we often try to 'sell' the gospel as something that makes our lives better – sort of like an additive to your car's gasoline.

But listen to Jesus' words:

If you try to keep your life for yourself, you will lose it. But if you

give up your life for my sake and for the sake of the Good News, you
will find true life. (Mark 8:35 – NLT)

Anyone who puts his love for father or mother above his love for me
does not deserve to be mine, and he who loves son or daughter more
than me is not worthy of me, and neither is the man who refuses to
take up his cross and follow my way. The man who has found his
own life will lose it, but the man who has lost it for my sake will find
it. (Matthew 10:37-39 – Phillips)

Whoever is not willing to carry the cross and follow me cannot be
my follower. (Luke 14:27 – NCV)

You see, it's just not about us.

It's about God.

Part of the cost of worship is that we must volitionally give up our focus
on ourselves. Henry Blackaby, in his book *Experiencing God,* brings a
unique perspective to the will of God (Henry T. Blackaby & Claude V.
King, *Experiencing God* [Nashville: Broadman & Homan Publishers,
1994]). He writes that we often pray that God would show us his will for
our lives as if our lives are the most important. Blackaby challenges our
view of the will of God to help us understand that we are created to serve
God. The essence of his will is that we fit into *his* broader purposes. If we
will not do the task that accomplishes his will, he will call someone else
to do it. God's will for our life is that we faithfully live a life of worship.
The tasks that God calls us to do accomplish his will.

So many of our prayers, though spoken to God, concentrate on us: "God,
bless us in this endeavour"; "Lord, would you bring healing to the
cancerous parts of my body"; "Father, would you help me to accomplish
my assignments well"; "Jesus, empower me with your Holy Spirit."

There is nothing unbiblical about any of these prayers. In fact, they are reflected in numerous prayers throughout the Bible. Scripture even tells us to bring our requests to God (Philippians 4:6). These are good prayers to pray. But notice the object of those prayers. Although they do recognize and honour God's ability to provide for his people they are basically focused on us – our needs, our wants, our desires.

The focus of true worship is not on us or our needs. The focus of true worship is on God.

Worship involves volitionally directing our thoughts, prayers, songs and actions to God. Scriptures say that we are to bless the Lord (Deuteronomy 8:10; Psalm 72:18; 134:1-2; etc.)! We are to lift our voices and our lives in praise to the God of our salvation. God invites our participation. He prompts us to worship in many ways. But the decision to worship is volitional.

Worship is not a spectator sport. It is not something we watch but something we participate in. God prompts us. We decide to act and then direct our praise towards God. Worship centres on Jesus who demonstrated the love of the Father and completed the purchase of our salvation with his death and resurrection.

Worship involves a giving of ourselves to God – allowing him to be the focus of our life and activity. Scripture is full of encouragements to give ourselves to God. 1 Chronicles 22:19a says, "Now give yourselves completely to obeying the LORD your God."

Reality check!

When we worship we die to our self and give everything to a living God. Worship costs us something.

In 2 Samuel 24 David is doing a census. Pretty ordinary, right?
But God had forbidden the kings to count the number of people available to fight in their army. You see, a census is a measurement of power. It's just logical. If you have a lot of warriors and your enemy only has a few, you have a better chance of winning.

There's a problem with that? (It all seems to make so much sense!) God asked his people to put their whole trust in him. Even though God had proven himself time and time again, the Israelites consistently turned their backs on trusting God and put their trust in human power.

David's sin had huge ramifications. God punished Israel. 70,000 people died in three days.

But the story has a great ending. David, referred to as a man after God's own heart, finally gets it. He goes up to the farmer, Araunah, and asks him to sell him his threshing floor and oxen so he can make a sacrifice to the Lord. Araunah offers his property free of charge but David insists on paying for it. He replies, "No, I insist on paying you for it. I will not sacrifice to the Lord my God burnt offerings that cost me nothing." (2 Samuel 24:24)

Worship costs us something. It involves a giving up of my rights and desires so that I might meet God's desire to be worshipped.

It's not just an Old Testament principle. Listen to what Jesus tells his disciples in Luke 9:62: "No one who puts his hand to the plough and looks back is fit for service in the kingdom of God."

Worship is sacrifice. God will ask a different sacrifice of each of his children. For some a sacrifice of worship may be using their body in worship through lifted hands or bended knees in obedience to what God is requiring of them – in spite of what others are doing. For some the sacrifice may be that they need to give up some of their personal free time in order to serve the needs of a neighbour who is going through a difficulty. For others the sacrifice might be to reject a great job offer to which God seems to be saying "No."

Worship is giving our lives to God and our fellow believers, seeking first his kingdom, fixing our eyes on the author and perfecter of our faith (1 John 3:16; Matthew 6:33; Hebrews 12:2). If we continue to look back, we lose our focus on who God is and what he is doing. When we are distracted by those things that don't point us to the object of our faith, we are not true worshippers.

But more than that, Jesus says we are not even fit for the kingdom of God.

Those are tough words! But God never said that following him would be easy – why would we expect that becoming better worshippers would be easy?

There are many things that distract us from worshipping God – family, work, gathering possessions, growing a business, entertainment, church – we each have our list. Ultimately, our true worship of God costs us more than our gifts and talents. True worship costs us our lives.

Not everyone who says to me,
'Lord, Lord,' will enter the kingdom of heaven,
but only he who does the will of my Father who is in heaven.
Many will say to me on that day,
'Lord, Lord, did we not prophesy in your name, and in your name drive out
demons and perform many miracles?'
Then I will tell them plainly, 'I never knew you. Away from me, you evildoers!'
Therefore everyone who hears these words of mine and puts them into practice
is like a wise man who built his house on the rock.
Matthew 7:21-24

CHAPTER FOUR

WE'RE USING OUR GIFTS – WHAT MORE DOES GOD WANT?
The sacrifice of worship

God wants YOU!

In Matthew 7:21-27, Jesus gives his disciples a revolutionary teaching. Just like us, the early followers of God wanted an easy measuring stick to evaluate their value in God's kingdom.

Having the right gifts and abilities, knowing the right phraseology, being known for powerful ministry – any of these things – do not make a worshipper! Frankly, God can do his work without us. He chooses to use us. He doesn't want our successful ministry and gifts – he wants our hearts. He wants our lives.

In 1987, when Jim Bakker's reputation and that of the PTL ministry fell apart and he was incarcerated, Jimmy Swaggart was purported to have been asked whether his ministry was in danger of falling as well. His apparent response was that his ministry would never fall because if it did, 90% of the world's evangelism would come to a screeching halt. Less than a year later his encounters with a prostitute became public knowledge and he and his ministry fell. And 90% of the world's evangelism didn't come to a screeching halt.

Surprised?

Let's get this straight. God longs for you to use your gifts for his work. His heart is broken by men and women who have started with a heart-filled passion for God and then lose it in the intensity of their ministry. We can never forget that even the words 'our ministry' are antithetical to a worshipper . . . it's never ours. We are *his* servants.

God cares more about a person than he cares about their ministry. No matter how well you are known. No matter how important your gifts and talents are. No matter how much 'ministry' happens. No matter how much adulation you receive from the church or society. If your personal life is not developing a closer relationship with God, if your talk is different from your walk, if your private life doesn't reflect a friendship with and passion for God – God isn't impressed. He will do whatever he needs to do to bring you to a place of repentance and restoration.

Dietrich Bonhoeffer, a Christian theologian and pastor who died at the hands of the Nazis, declared in his book *The Cost of Discipleship,* "When Christ calls a man (to follow him), he bids him come and die" (Dietrich Bonhoeffer, *The Cost of Discipleship* [New York: Macmillan Publishing, 1963] p. 99). Following Jesus is not about pampering the self-will. It is about putting self-will to death. Christ does not offer us self-fulfillment, but crucifixion. Paradoxically, when we truly follow Jesus in this way, there is true joy, freedom and abundant life. In losing our life, we gain life.

Isn't that what Jesus was saying in the Gospels about leaving everything behind so that you might ultimately find what is worth having? In Mark 8:34–35 Jesus "called the crowd to him along with his disciples and said: 'If anyone would come after me, he must deny himself and take up his cross and follow me. For whoever wants to save his life will lose it, but whoever loses his life for me and for the gospel will save it.'"

Following Jesus is not a simple thing of just saying 'yes' to his offer of salvation! It begins there but the journey to becoming like Jesus is filled with sacrifice of self so that he might be glorified.

I will not offer to the Lord a sacrifice that costs me nothing.

Our life with Christ is based upon a covenant. And every covenant has two sides to it. On the one side are the things Christ covenants that he will do for us: to love us with an everlasting love, to forgive us of all our sins, to speak to us, to lead and guide us all our days, to prepare a place for us to dwell with him for eternity, to empower us with his Holy Spirit so we can defeat the enemy.

On the other side is what he asks of us: to lay down our lives for him, to die to our self-will, to seek first his kingdom, to forcefully take hold of the kingdom, to lose our lives for the sake of the gospel, to make all relationships secondary to him.

In fact, Jesus was so committed to this covenant that he willingly laid down his life on a cross for us. And he is so committed to the covenant that he reminds us that the cost of that commitment for him is no less than what he requires of us. In essence, discipleship is death – dying to ourselves and living for Christ. So much so that he says in Luke 14:27 that "anyone who does not carry his cross and follow me cannot be my disciple." A true act of worship for a disciple is to lay down their life in preference to the One who laid down his for them. Each day a disciple works to fulfill their covenant with their Lord and Saviour by picking up their cross and following Jesus. Each day they invite Jesus to participate with them in whatever activity they do and look to participate in those things they see him doing.

I will not offer to the Lord a sacrifice that costs me nothing.

Our sacrifice of worship needs to be more than what happens on a Sunday morning. As important as that is to our worship practice and experience, our worship needs to move beyond Sunday worship services, worship songs and worship events. Our worship needs to intersect with our lives – our walk – because God desires to intersect with our lives, totally.

As I have studied and taught and attempted to live as a worship walker every day with God, he has surprised me in many ways with how he desires to communicate with me. He has surprised me with the variety of ways he has invited me to interact with him. He has encouraged me to worship him in whatever activity I am participating in. He has opened my eyes to see him and all his glory in the smallest of things, events and occurrences.

My desire with this book is not to provide you with a step by step 'here's how to' journal of learning to live as a worship walker each day with God. My desire is not to stop or to discourage the use of music in worshipping God. I love music and I love to worship God through music. I love to lead others into worship through music. But I don't want us to stay in the place where worship equals music. My desire is that through this book we will be able to begin a journey of exploration – exploring all the ways that God makes himself known to us everyday so that we might always be aware of his presence and always be living in an attitude of praise and worship to the Lover of our souls.

There have been many things which have helped me to explore a multiplicity of ways to enjoy worshipping God each day. I share them with you not so much as steps to follow but as suggestions to 'jump-start' you in discovering the wealth of worshipping God with every breath, with every step.

And so, in these next chapters you will find written the expressions of my journey of discovering how God can receive our worship and praise each day. My journey is such a small fragment of what God can do and is doing, but I pray that it will stimulate your hearts and minds to broaden your worship expression and experience.

Worship is for God. Let's not limit ourselves in this world as we anticipate an eternity worshipping in his presence in the next. As we walk, let's learn how to recognize where worship and life intersect everyday.

$\mathcal{P}$ART 2

Walking it out . . .

I keep asking that the God of our Lord Jesus Christ, the glorious Father,
may give you the spirit of wisdom and revelation,
so that you may know him fully.
I pray also that the eyes of your heart may be enlightened
in order that you may know the hope to which he has called you,
the riches of his glorious inheritance in the saints,
and his incomparably great power for us who believe.
Ephesians 1:17-19a

CHAPTER FIVE

A SPIRIT OF WISDOM AND REVELATION
Discovering all that God has given us

Paul prayed that God would give the Ephesians a spirit of wisdom and revelation so that they would know Christ fully. To know Christ fully! To know him as we are known by him! How I pray for the same full knowledge of Christ for today's church!

If Paul was anything, he was passionate in his relationship with Jesus. His desire was that all would come to know this Messiah – this Saviour. His prayer for the churches he planted along his journeys hinted at a desire that they would outstrip him in their passionate pursuit of knowing Jesus. And his prayer called upon the heavenly Father to grant a gift to his church – a gift of wisdom and revelation.

But this request wasn't necessarily for revealing spiritual truths. Nor was it for gaining great wisdom for people to stand and marvel at. Paul's desire was that God would present his church with a spirit of wisdom and revelation so that they would know their Lord Jesus Christ – their Saviour – to the fullest.

Jesus had said earlier that when he left the world he would send a Comforter who would lead his church into all truth and would help them to understand everything that Christ taught (John 14:15-17). And at Pentecost he sent his Holy Spirit upon his people.

The Holy Spirit gives us the ability to see Christ in places where we might otherwise miss his presence. The Holy Spirit gives us the ability to see God's presence and activity in nature, friends, strangers and many, many unexpected places – if we are willing to listen and observe.

As we pray along with Paul for a desire of a spirit of wisdom and revelation, the Holy Spirit begins to activate our senses and our desires, propelling us into that direction of discovering and knowing God fully.

To 'know God fully' is much more than just gathering information about him. It is a knowing of his person, his passion and his presence within the context of relationship. It is a knowing of his desires, his intentions. It is a knowing of what his plans are – for us – for others. Knowing Christ helps us to worship and serve him with clarity, understanding who he is and who he is calling us to be ("for we shall be like him" – 1 John 3:2).

If you fully know Christ, then you will know his deepest desires and intentions. Something like marriage. I thought I knew my wife Gayle when I married her. Wow! Was I surprised! Although I knew part of who she was, as our relationship grew over the years I began to realize what a complex and profound person she is. As we learned to understand one another and listen to each other, I began to know her more fully, understanding the depth of her character.

In a good marriage, as you come to more fully know each other, you attempt to please each other based upon what you know of your spouse. The ideal of a marriage relationship is to relate to each other at the deepest level – truly knowing one another. Partners open up to know each other's heart, desires, longings and aspirations. The relationship grows and matures as they begin to have full knowledge of each other.

Our human marriages are imperfect examples of 'knowing' as God uses it. Yet marriage, as one of our most intimate human relationships, is a good model of the process of knowing God. Just like the effort we make to get to know our spouse, we need to make a deliberate effort to seek God and mature in our relationship with him as well.

In this postmodern world, we are at the best place for truly understanding what it means to 'know' God. Our confusion about living our life fully knowing God, has been perpetuated by a lingering penchant for scientific knowledge left over from our modernist forebearers. 'Knowing' isn't an accumulated list of data or information. It's much deeper than that. It's understanding that there is knowledge beyond science and that no knowledge is pure within itself. It's understanding that knowing God cannot be neatly compartmentalized in a segment of our person, but it invades every part of us.

God promises to reveal the truth to us if we seek him faithfully. James 1:5 prompts us to ask for wisdom: "If any of you lacks wisdom, he should ask God, who gives generously to all without finding fault, and it will be given to him."

Our desire should be for an ever-expanding understanding of the depths to which Christ has called us. He promises that the Holy Spirit will guide us into those depths. Paul reminds the Corinthians that " . . . we did not receive the spirit of the world, but we received the Spirit that is from God *so that we can know all that God has given us*" (1 Corinthians 2:12 – emphasis added).

My wife Gayle loves to give Christmas gifts. She loves to wrap them in wonderful splashes of coloured paper, ribbons and bows. To be honest, they are often works of art that are gifts in and of themselves. But the wrapping is only a sample of what is yet to come. The wrapping, though beautiful, is only the 'teaser' for what awaits to be discovered within.

How I pray that each of us, as worshippers, would have a wrapping that is only a teaser of the beauty that is within us! Yet, too often, it's just the opposite. The beautiful package is all there is. Some of us are like the Sardis church. Listen to Jesus' message: "I know what you are doing; I know that you have the reputation of being alive, even though you are dead" (Revelation 3:1).

Ouch!

Many Christians have built a beautiful cloak of 'godliness'.

Others have honestly received the gift of salvation – forgiveness of their sin and the recognition of the lordship of Jesus Christ. They speak with stirring words about how Christ rescued them from the brink of death. They weep at the precious thought of being with him for eternity. They encourage others to accept this free gift of salvation with which they can enter the heavenly kingdom when they die. They have received the gift of salvation. Yet they are living with a package that has not yet been opened to the gift inside. They live their lives holding on to that gift without discovering the depth of what God has also provided deep inside.

It's like Gayle giving me a wonderfully wrapped Christmas gift. I receive it with awe and wonder. I recite glowing words of how beautiful it looks and how she has really outdone herself this year. And then I place it on the fireplace mantel and tell all our guests who come over, "Look at the beautiful gift Gayle gave me for Christmas this year! Isn't it absolutely amazing? I just love her so much for her thoughtfulness."

Well, I'm quite sure that Gayle would be pretty quick to say, "Gareth, just cut the crap and open it!"

When we said "Yes" to Jesus' offer of salvation, he gave us several gifts. One, he forgave us our sins. He cleansed us from our unrighteousness, making us acceptable in his sight. Two, he made us heirs to his kingdom – children of God. Three, he gave us gifts with which to serve him and others. Four, he gave us his Holy Spirit – his presence living within us.

The first two gifts just are. We are forgiven – even when we act like we're not or when we have trouble understanding grace. We are God's children – even when we act like we don't know him.

The third gift is tough. We are often confused about talents and gifts and just how it all plays out in our daily lives. Talents are part of our DNA. They are 'gifts' that the Creator gave us at the time of our creating. As his children, we should use our talents to the glory of God. Gifts are God-given for use in the building of his kingdom. I know a woman who is a great teacher. She loves to be in front of a class and has honed her skills well. But she is very quick to say that teaching is not her spiritual gift. It's a God-given talent. When I pushed her, she explained to me that she has the gift of prophecy. There are times, when for no reason, she knows that the Holy Spirit is giving her a message for the church. That's her gift.

Finally, the gift of the Holy Spirit is a treasure that I am just beginning to understand. The Spirit is our guide in learning about all that God has given us. He helps us to dig past the surface into the depths of God. Yes, God has given us salvation. Hallelujah! But there is a whole lot more that God has given to us in our 'package' of salvation which waits to be discovered. He wants to show us and will show us all these things as we allow the Holy Spirit to guide us into the journey of discovering all that God has prepared for those he loves.

Worship of God invokes the Spirit's activity in our lives to help us press into his depths. Worship draws our attention from ourselves to God enabling us to begin to see things from his perspective, encouraging us to open up to his correction and inviting us to follow his leadership in our lives. Worship helps us to be open for God's revelation of himself to us. Living lives of worship equips us with tools to dig deeply into understanding who God is and all that he has prepared for those he loves.

Ultimately, worship tunes our heart, our eyes and our ears to feel, see and hear God.

And when God reveals more of himself to us, we are changed to be more like him. He helps us to respond to life situations with his wisdom. He becomes more and more our focus for living.

I struggle to open myself to God each day. In reality, some days it's tough and the issues of life get in the way. But here are a few things I do to help me focus on God:

1. Ask God for wisdom every day.

   This forces me to articulate my dependence on God and tell him that I need him. I invite God to speak into my everyday situations. I regularly pray in faith: "Lord, you have told us that if we lack wisdom we should pray for it, because you give generously and graciously" (see James 1:5).

2. Look for ways to give God the opportunity to reveal himself.

   Sometimes days go by where I haven't seen a trace of God. Then I stop and realize that I haven't even called him or looked for him. Seeing God is active, not passive. Wouldn't it be nice if God just popped an email to me to tell me more about him. Or like Saul, that he would literally stop me and tell me where he wants me to go. But while occasionally God comes to me in a miraculous and stunning way, most times I see God in day-to-day things.

3. Take time to talk to other believers. WOW – no matter where they are on their journey, their faith changes me.

I ask them how they see God and how God interacts with them. I resist trying to duplicate their experience. Knowing that God speaks into people's lives is fantastic. Because God is not a pre-programmed machine, he will speak differently to each of his children.

By far the most difficult challenge is to trust. Growing up in a Mennonite home has got me entrenched in a stoic belief that I have to do it on my own. Each of us has our own past that challenges our ideas of faith. Some days trust comes so easy. Other days, I have to walk forward, in faith, trusting that God is there in the silence. I believe God wants me to discover more about him.

4. Every so often look back.

Modern Christians are missing much of God's blessing by doing away with the Passover. In the Jewish tradition, the Passover was a time of telling the story of God's faithfulness. Family, children and friends gathered together and reminded each other that God was faithful, even in their most difficult times. As I remember the many ways God has been faithful, I know that he will continue to be faithful.

Be still before the LORD and wait patiently for him.
Psalm 37:7

Be still, and know that I am God.
Psalm 46:10

CHAPTER SIX

SILENCE
A tool of worship

I snore.

It's a flaw in my physical make-up that I have no control over. I can go to bed convincing myself that I will not snore or wear those silly little nostril expanders and my wife Gayle still pokes me in the side in the middle of the night.

I've been a part of a North American committee for my denomination and have been at meetings in different parts of Canada and the United States together with 15 other committee members. When it comes time to divvy up hotel rooms, I always get put together with the other two or three snorers! To make things worse, they all seem to be able to fall asleep the moment their heads hit the pillow. Now, Gayle would tell you that I have been known to have that same trait, but when it is absolutely necessary for me to fall asleep before others (as in the case with my two or three snoring roommates), I can't seem to do it!

But I found these neat silicone putty earplugs which effectively shut out a majority of the disturbing cacophony. Silence . . . I can fall asleep. So now I always travel with my earplugs – in planes, hotels, peoples' homes. And if others can't sleep because of my snoring? Let them get their own earplugs!

We live in a noisy world. From the time the radio alarm clock wakes us up, to the conclusion of the network newscast, our lives are filled with sound. On our way to work or to pick up groceries we listen to the radio, tape, or CD. While in high school, our oldest son Chris claimed that he couldn't really concentrate on his studies unless he was in front of the TV or was listening to music. Things have changed since I had high school homework! Even at night – while our three grown children were still living at home – Gayle and I would often go to bed with 'trance', 'break-beat' and 'house' music emanating through our bedroom walls from our oldest son's computer music compositions.

In our modern, noisy world we're not used to silence at any time. A couple of years ago we went back to the farm for a vacation and had a hard time going to sleep because it was so quiet! We finally borrowed my brother-in-law's fan so that we could at least have some 'white noise' just so we could fall asleep!

Yet the noise is more than just a product of our technological and machine orientated society. Noise helps take away the pain and discomfort of silence. We want to fill up the silence with sound or activity. We are so used to noise that we have to have background noise. When we are alone at home, we turn on the TV or radio – even if we're not watching or listening – just to fill the house with sound.

Silence scares us. It doesn't seem natural. Sometimes I wonder if we are so afraid of what we might hear in the silence that we refuse to allow it. Or perhaps we are afraid that we will hear nothing at all.

The Psalmist says, "Be still, and know that I am God" (Psalm 46:10). The suggestion is that we must pause in our very busy, very noisy lives so that we can hear God.

Our desire of 'no dead air' has changed our worship. We want the program to be fast, efficient and keep our attention. We are a generation that was raised on two minute sound bites. Sesame Street was brilliant at it!

Our churches have slowly evolved to exclude silence as well. Even the tiny breaks of silence while we waited for the next person to come up to the front for Scripture reading or announcements or a song have been replaced with people waiting 'in the wings' so that no time is 'wasted', waiting in silence.

There was a time when silence and reflection was part of a church worship experience. There was time for meditation on a Scripture passage, time for silent prayer, time to allow God to speak. That's becoming a rarity. I think it's mostly because we really don't know how to use silence.

I'm sure you can identify with me when I say how frustrating it is when there is silence during times of prayer. In fact, it happens many times when I am in small groups and prayer meetings. When the leader asks for 'two or three to pray and then he'll close', I will often jump in and pray if no one else does if there are more than 30 seconds of silence.

Why?

I'm uncomfortable with silence. And so I pray – more to remove the silence than that I have anything particular I need to say to God at that moment – especially in public prayer. I assure myself that it is because I am comfortable with praying out loud in public and I don't want others to feel uncomfortable or pressured into having to pray because of the oppressive weight silence seems to bring to the group.

But can our propensity to fill every waking moment with sound and activity mitigate against our ability to find a place of worship within the silence? Does our 'noise' interfere with something God desires for us that can only be found within silence? Can our worship include inactivity, solitude, quietness, reflection, meditation, listening?

More than anything else, silence gives us the chance to hear God. Remember Elijah being instructed to go stand on the mountain in the presence of the Lord (1 Kings 19:11-13)? From this passage we begin to understand, intellectually at least, the importance of silence in hearing the Lord's voice. Elijah looked for the Lord in the power of the storm, in the might of the earthquake and in the consuming heat of the fire. But God was not in these powerful forces. He came in a whisper, a breath barely perceivable – a still, small voice.

Silence is not a comfortable part of our world. We are pressured to keep up with our culture and the norms of our society. The glitz and professionalism of the movies and entertainment is being absorbed by our churches. And it's a dilemma. Why would someone come to church if the entertainment isn't as good as at our entertainment centres?

Well, the obvious answer would be to find God . . . but let's refuse sarcasm for a moment. The pressure to entertain people by programs is huge. Our little church, planted in the middle of a high immigrant, low income area, is struggling to understand what it means to be a church. We talk in circles about becoming a part of the community. But we're still tempted to put on 'one more program' so that the people will come to us – even though we know that our calling is to go and live among the people so that they too will know the glory of our God as we work alongside of them in the community.

As Christians, we feel that we are competing against the world for air time. Naturally, our logic is, the church should be giving people something that can compare with the world's entertainment.

But we have it wrong! I know I'm yelling but I can't stress this enough: THE CHURCH SHOULD BE GIVING PEOPLE SOMETHING MUCH, MUCH BETTER THAN THEY COULD GET ANYWHERE ELSE!

And that might just be the opportunity for silence.

We seldom give ourselves the opportunity to 'centre down', to quiet our busy lives, to sit patiently waiting for the Lord to draw near and speak in his 'still, small voice'. That's something that seems best left for our private times of devotion . . . if we can actually do so without falling asleep!

A number of years ago, I was leading worship at a conference in western Canada. On the second night of the conference I became keenly aware of God's presence drawing near. In fact, I didn't use the final two songs in the worship package the team and I had rehearsed earlier because there was a clear sense that God had 'drawn near'. I stood on stage in silence for a couple of minutes, then put my guitar away and sat down. The band followed suit and also came and sat down.

For the next 75 minutes we sat in silence. David Damien, the guest speaker for the conference, never got up to speak. No announcements were made. We just sat in silence.

It was an amazing process I went through during that time of quiet. First, I thought, "Wow, this is really neat! An awesome, unplanned time of quiet to reflect on what God has been saying to us through the songs we've been singing." But twenty minutes later, I began to question whether I should have maybe done those last two or three songs anyway. Or maybe I should get up and play again – you know – to fill the silence. Maybe just add some 'mood' background music. Forty-five minutes into this time of quiet reflection, the silence had become excruciatingly painful as my thoughts began a valiant effort to fill the void with sound. "Didn't they fly this guy up here to speak? So what is he getting paid for? We came to hear him speak! The church is not getting its money's worth! The people attending this conference are getting ripped off!"

Finally, for the last fifteen minutes – my resistance finally worn thin – I was able to become quiet before the Lord and begin to listen for his voice. And he made his still, small voice heard.

After this time of silence, the guest speaker stood up and asked the congregation what God had been saying to them. People stood up to share what they had heard God speak to them during that time of silence.

God had spoken in powerful ways during the silence.

When I walk into the cathedrals of Europe, I am drawn to the echoing silence of the stone walls. There are many factors that give the feeling of awesomeness: the age of the building; the height of the ceilings, the art work, the architecture, the stained glass. But more than that, there is a sense of quiet reflection. People enter into the building talk in hushed whispers.

While I love the excited voices in our church on Sunday morning, sometimes I wonder if we need to provide a public place where those who need to listen to God can just come and be quiet, where there is an expectation of silence.

God used silence in the past to speak to his people. He uses silence today to speak to us. Are we taking time to become silent before him so we might more clearly hear and understand his voice? Sometimes our best worship starts when we become silent and wait for his still, small voice to speak.

I have been on three-day retreats of complete silence. It's a wonderful experience! I've been in church services where the words were taken from me and there is simply silence as we wait for God. I have sat with grieving friends and family where silence is the only comforter.

Yet I still get caught in the noisy activity of my world. I still let the clutter of noise overwhelm the voice of God. Yet I long to find God in the silence. Here are a few of the things that I do:

1. Try to find specific times for silence.

   One thing I've learned is that I am really programmed for noise. It's usually best if I find silence in a place I don't usually work. A walk in the woods is great – but it's not always practical. In our house, the best place for silence is the living room. We rarely use it except for company and it is usually free from the clutter of daily living. My office is the worst place for silence. It's cluttered with the work I have left undone, so it's pretty tough to settle my heart and my mind.

2. Learn to anticipate distractions.

   I try not to feel guilty and simply acknowledge that finding a place of silence is tough for me. I often have a pen and paper with me when I'm spending time alone with God. The first fifteen minutes are often filled with many thoughts of what I 'have to remember to do' that day. If I don't write them down they will continue to distract me throughout my quiet time.

3. Learn to enjoy the silence.

I'm not all that patient. I figure that if I have given God 30 minutes to show up, he should be on time. But you know what? God isn't working on my time line. He is waiting for me to come to him without the clutter I bring to the meeting. I'm learning to appreciate the silence even if God doesn't reveal himself in any significant way. It's nice just to sit alone with him.

When I first left my job as youth pastor in anticipation of where God was to lead me next, I spent each Thursday in the basement of a friend's church. He was the only one who knew I was down there so I had many uninterrupted hours together with God. I would often lie facedown on the floor before God and wait for him to speak in the silence. And I would often fall asleep.

At first I was troubled by my falling asleep and not being awake to 'listen' at all times. But God encouraged me that he enjoyed my time with him and that, if I was tired, I should not be anxious about sleeping. We would just continue on when I awoke. Or sometimes he would just encourage me in my sleep in a variety of ways.

4. Try to wait for others when they are in prayer or in thought.

Like I said, I don't really like the silent pauses in corporate prayer – it makes me feel that people aren't participating. But I am learning to deal with the silence. I try not to be too anxious to end a time of quiet because I don't know what God is revealing to my brother or sister. Sometimes it is these times of silence that allow God to break through. I try to give God an opportunity to speak. Then I try to take time to ask what people hear God speaking to them in the quiet. I'm often surprised when I hear the things God is saying to his people.

5. Try to make time for silence in unusual times and places.

How instinctive to get in the car and turn up the radio (or turn it down if Gayle's been driving)! But it doesn't have to be that way. Before I leave on a trip, I rush around to get the right CDs to listen to. But lately I've been turning off the CD player, leaving the radio alone and driving in silence. It gives me a significant time in which to enjoy the Lord's presence, think about my day and the moments or hours that flow through my fingers. Sometimes a small time of disruption from the normal pattern of life gives God the opportunity to speak.

Take a break from worship music. Learn to love and worship Jesus in the quiet. He is there too.

In that day you will no longer ask me anything.
I tell you the truth,
my Father will give you whatever you ask in my name.
John 16:23

CHAPTER SEVEN

ASKING
So that the Son may bring glory to the Father

My wife is a communicator and does a lot of work with fundraisers. She has a unique twist on the power of asking! She often talks about the arrogance of sufficiency in our society. Many Christian organizations come to her and ask for help in fundraising, but they don't want it to sound like they're asking for funds! While the thought of asking in a way that doesn't convey that one is asking seems somewhat askew, I wonder if our wealth, independence and lack of real need in our society and in our churches has driven away the desire to ask.

A few years ago, a friend of ours had an African man and his son stay with him. They were here by the grace of God and the compassion of a few individuals. The son desperately needed heart surgery and could not have that surgery in his own country. They were refugees and lived in complete poverty. The man noticed that the family had a sewing machine in the house and, as odd as it seemed, no one used it. It just sat well-oiled and ready to be used in a closet in the spare room. So he asked if he could have it. He knew that he could take it to his village and use it to earn an income that would feed his family. A sewing machine like that would cost a whole year's wage in his country.

Our North American friend was taken aback. He noticed that this man had little hesitation in asking for something that he needed. He simply saw what he needed and he asked for it.

To those of us in North America, it seems a little greedy! But it wasn't at all. This was a man with great need. While in Canada, he saw a people with great wealth. He saw homes with so many things, things that they rarely used. Surely these people with such a great capacity to give would give generously.

Jesus says:

> *Which of you, if his son asks for bread, will give him a stone? Or if he asks for a fish, will give him a snake? If you, then, though you are evil, know how to give good gifts to your children, how much more will your Father in heaven give good gifts to those who ask him!* (Matthew 7:9-11)

Our kids are grown up, more or less. The spring of 2004 I went to Halifax to help my daughter move into her first apartment. It was a crummy little one-bedroom and had all the trappings of student housing. I was so proud of her – just finishing first year Nursing and struggling to pay for her Nursing degree and living expenses – she combed the garage sales for the least grimy couch, a couple of old vinyl chairs and a dresser. I wanted to buy her everything she needed!

How much more does God want to pour out his gifts on his children! God our Father loves to give good gifts to us, his children. He invites us to ask for that which we need. He promises to assist us when we need help. He WANTS us to ask.

When we ask, we acknowledge our need for God. We admit that we are not sufficient in and of ourselves. In my personal walk, I am not able to accomplish a life of worship. I need the Holy Spirit's prompting, power and passion to become a worshipper. This dependency, like hunger, will be satisfied with nothing less than that ". . . he must become greater and greater and I must become less and less" (John 3:30 – NLT).

One of the most difficult issues of worship is that I need to focus beyond the things that I think I want and need. I am so earthly! It's nearly impossible for me to imagine God – to imagine a heavenly focus. But I need to look beyond that which I know and ask God to give me a focus for him.

I need a focus to help me recognize my need – my utter dependency on God – a dependency that urges me to daily make God my all in all. I need a focus that reminds me that I am a citizen of another kingdom, living for a heavenly reward. I need to ask God to refocus my thinking so that I can worship him with my life.

But doesn't 'asking' really fit into prayer, not worship?

Yes, of course, but that doesn't separate itself from worship. Your whole life – including your prayer life – needs to be bathed in an attitude of worship. When you ask in your prayers, you acknowledge God. You tell God that you are completely and utterly dependent on him. Your prayers extend worth to God because he is the one from whom you expect to receive. You are placing trust in him to be able to provide for what you are requesting.

Asking requires an admission of real need. We need a provider because we are unable to provide for ourselves. That admission is an act of worship because it elevates God to a position of being our 'Jireh' – our Provider.

Six times in the Gospel of John (11:22; 14:14; 15:7,16; 16:23-24), Jesus reminds the disciples that the Father will give them whatever they ask in his name. Why? "So that the Son may bring glory to the Father" (John 14:13). God expects us to ask, because when he answers, it brings glory to his name.

The admission of our need becomes harder the more independent we become. As long as I have a well paying, secure job with all my physical needs met and a good amount stashed away for retirement, I don't really need God to be my 'Jireh'. As long as my family and friendships are in good order, I don't really need God to be my 'Jireh'. Now I'm not saying that, therefore, we should become destitute and disenfranchised with our family and friends in order to allow God to be our 'Jireh'. I'm simply stating that the more independent we are in this life, the more we need to be diligent in remaining dependent on God. Otherwise, we risk robbing him of his glory.

During the first few years of my ministry things were tight financially. There was plenty of work to be done, but not enough income coming in to provide me with a salary. Not until my fourth year in ministry did I begin to receive a half-time salary. During the second year Gayle began to work half-time which eventually grew into a full-time position. This took a lot of stress off the financial part of our lives and allowed us to begin to reduce our significant personal debt-load.

After her fourth year at a job that paid a good salary and benefits, she began to strongly sense God's nudging her to leave and to begin her own business. I was not really enthusiastic about the prospect of another risk. We had just started to get on our feet financially. A regular income was a good thing! When Gayle told me that she was seriously thinking of quitting her job and going on her own, I just couldn't accept it.

Then God gave me a dream (and I seldom have receive meaningful dreams) which confirmed several prophetic encouragements Gayle had received from others. There was little doubt that the little nudge we felt was being confirmed. But I didn't want to let go.

I was convinced that we would go bankrupt and lose everything if Gayle started this business. Not because God couldn't provide, but because I couldn't bring myself to trust that he wanted to give good gifts to his children. I couldn't even bring myself to ask God to build faith within me for that which I couldn't envision. And I fought hard against following God in this act of obedience he was asking my wife to take.

Finally, I had to come to a point of acknowledging God's lordship in my life and willingly follow him even if I couldn't see the sense in it. I had to be willing to say with Job: "Though he slay me, yet will I trust in him" (Job 13:15 – KJV). Instead of complaining about what I thought I was about to lose, I began to ask God to build faith in me for what he could accomplish for Gayle, for our family and for the glory of his name.

God began to give me faith for what he was about to accomplish. Six years later as I write this book, I can testify, to the glory of God, that he has not only sustained us, but he has increased his provision for Gayle's business and for us as a family.

But it's much, much more than income and financial benefits. When we are faithful, God gives us joy. And wherever we can, we want to share of the goodness of the Lord with whomever God brings into our path. To him be the glory and the honour for he proved himself to be Jehovah Jireh – the Lord, our Provider.

Another part of extending our worship to God is agreeing with what he desires to do in us and through us. God uses our worship to draw others to himself. Psalm 2:8 says: "Ask of me, and I will make the nations your inheritance, the ends of the earth your possession." Our lives of worship to God are beacons of light through which his gospel is revealed to others. Part of asking God for the nations involves allowing him to shine through us so that his works of righteousness in us are visible to those who observe us.

> And even if our gospel is veiled, it is veiled to those who are perishing. . . . For God, who said, 'Let light shine out of darkness,' made his light shine in our hearts to give us the light of the knowledge of the glory of God in the face of Christ. (2 Corinthians 4:3-6)

We need to recognize that God will use our lives of worship to draw others to himself. In our church, *The Dwelling Place*, about 40% of the people in attendance are refugees. People, who have escaped from countries of violence and abuse to seek refuge in Canada, have found themselves within our small church. Not everyone has a personal relationship with Jesus. Some faith commitments have been to other religions or have been completely non-existent. But as the people, called to serve in this little church, embrace the cross of Jesus Christ in their daily living, and as they give of themselves in unconditional love for others, the Holy Spirit is bringing faith, hope, love and life to people from many nations.

Asking God for his provision, his wisdom and his gifts is foundational to the beginnings and the growth of this little church. One of the things we constantly bring before God is asking him to open the hearts of the internationals living in our city. God is transforming lives, in the Victoria Hills region of Kitchener and beyond, as believers begin to ask God for the nations and live lives of worship to him. Some have demonstrated their devotion to God and the vision for reaching people in Victoria Hills by selling their homes and moving into this area so that they can live in the neighbourhood, allowing their love of Jesus to shine through their relationships. And God is bringing people to himself as they respond to the friendship, love and acceptance they are experiencing.

When our worship includes asking in accordance with God's will and purpose, we connect with his power. The power of God then infuses our worship and prayers. And God acts. This is also where asking and corporate worship come together. As Jesus says in Matthew 18:19-20: "Again, I tell you that if two of you on earth agree about anything you ask for, it will be done for you by my Father in heaven. For where two or three come together in my name, there am I with them." Sometimes he acts to motivate us with creative energies to accomplish the answer (or part of the answer). Sometimes he acts by moving through others' lives in a way that opens them up to his work in them. Sometimes he acts miraculously. When we ask, we will receive. And the Son gives glory to the Father.

Here are some principles I've learned in regard to asking:

1. Ask God to prepare you to listen to his voice as you get yourself ready for worship. Asking heightens your awareness of what you are getting set to do. It helps you focus on worshipping God.

2. Ask the Holy Spirit to speak. Invite him to speak to you about those things that God wants to work in you. Invite him to reveal his visions and dreams for your life. Ask God to reveal his love for the nations and how you can be a part of showing the glory of God through your life.

3. Ask him to help you to listen. Sometimes we need help to listen as we often become distracted in our worship walk. Be willing to respond to what the Spirit is saying. Write down those visions and dreams he brings to mind, regarding your service to him, in your relationships and your areas of work. Reflect on what he is showing you and what you might do to help implement those things.

4. Regularly ask God to fulfill those visions and dreams for his honour and glory. Jesus taught the disciples a parable in Luke 18:1 (NLT) " . . . to illustrate their need for constant prayer and to show them that they must never give up." Be persistent. Be focused. Be tenacious! Don't let a vision die just because it takes a long time to be fulfilled.

I remember a communion service a number of years ago when Peter Fehderau, an elderly friend of mine who has since gone to be with the Lord, stood up during a testimony time to give praise to God because a friend of his, for whom he had been praying for 25 years, had given his heart to the Lord that week. I jumped up in enthusiasm yelling, "Yes!" Talk about perseverance! That's the tenacity and diligence Jesus was talking about. Don't give up! Keep asking!

5. Believe that God is receiving glory and worship as he hears your requests and then brings about the answers to them. Not only do we celebrate when our requests are answered, but God celebrates with us and he receives glory and praise because of those answers.

6. Bring your intercession into your corporate worship times. "Everything you ask for in prayer, if you have faith, you will receive" (Matthew 21:22 – Phillips)! Sharing the burden of prayer with brothers and sisters in the Lord increases a community spirit of worship and lightens the burden of prayer. "Many hands make light work" – in prayer as well as in physical work. Also, shared prayer brings about shared blessing when those prayers are answered. God is pleased to see a body of believers labouring together in prayer and intercession for a common purpose that he has laid on their hearts.

After the earthquake came a fire,
but the LORD was not in the fire.
And after the fire came a gentle whisper.
When Elijah heard it, he pulled his cloak over his face
and went out and stood at the mouth of the cave.
Then a voice said to him, 'What are you doing here, Elijah?'
1 Kings 19:12-13

CHAPTER EIGHT

KNOWING AND OBEYING HIS PROMPTING

Listening to the voice of the Holy Spirit

Elijah had just come off a great high. Living in a land that dismissed the God of creation, the people had turned to idols. The most popular one being Baal. Elijah, totally trusting God, had set up a bit of a circus display and he called on God to do his thing. And God did – with a bang. While Baal refused to set the sacrifice on fire no matter how loud the people called, God's voice thundered in the mountains. And he honoured Elijah's faith by consuming the sacrifice in a fire so hot that even the bricks burned.

Then Elijah had a bit of a downturn. He had just heard AND seen God. Then he ran. As he waited, he felt an earthquake. But it wasn't God. A fire came down. But that wasn't God either. Then, softly, a whisper of wind held the voice of God (1 Kings 19:11-13).

In order for Elijah to hear God's voice, he had to shut out the noise around him and listen. He was away from the everyday, normal activities of his life. He was away from people. He was away from the things he knew. And he was a little scared.

While this story is only one way God speaks (after all, Balaam was stopped in the middle of a road and God spoke through his donkey – Numbers 22:28), I think we can learn a lot from it.

First of all, Elijah was able to discern God's voice. He was able to tell when God spoke. He didn't recognize the timbre or the format – that surprised him. But he knew God well enough to be able to discern when it was God who spoke. He was also discerning enough to listen.

Secondly, God is not predictable. Elijah expected God to speak in the earthquake and the fire. Those were ways in which he had spoken before. It was hard to understand God speaking in a still, small voice. God was always equated with loud, big, powerful. We need to be prepared for God to speak in ways that are unexpected. We need to know his voice so well, that whether he speaks in the fire or the earthquake or in a still, small voice, we are able to hear him.

Recently I was out in mid-western Canada working with a Discipleship School. God did some awesome things one evening with the students and leaders during a worship time.

We had an awesome worship and ministry time with a good number of the students experiencing a touch of God in a deeper way – praying for each other, confessing their sins and fears, etc.

One girl was looking completely lost and discouraged. I went and asked her how she was doing. She said, "I'm okay." I shook my head and said, "No, you're not!" and she welled up with tears.

The Lord gave me a bit of insight and three words that described her condition – fear, confusion and guilt. She broke down crying, saying that she didn't know how to hear God or feel him and that he just never seemed real to her at all. She also said that she was dealing with some personal issues that she just wasn't yet ready to talk to anyone about, but she really wanted to hear from God on it. I prayed with her and told her that sometimes we limit God's communication with us because we expect God to speak to us the same way he speaks to others. But sometimes God speaks to us through events and occurrences that might seem coincidental at first, when often it is God wanting to communicate with us and encourage us with his presence.

The following morning she went out for a run at 6:30 a.m. A deer fawn had run out onto the road, stopped, looked at her and then bounded off into the woods. She didn't think much about it initially but as she ran past the spot where the deer had stopped, she remembered our conversation the evening before. She stopped running and looked back to where the deer had entered the woods – hoping to perhaps get another look at it – perhaps to understand something of what God might be wanting to communicate to her through this incident. What she saw, at the side of the road where the deer had crossed, was a large sign made up of stones forming the word **FREEDOM** in bold letters. She broke down weeping, knowing that God had spoken to her through the deer and the sign – indicating that there was freedom that God wanted to bring to her. Later on, in Guatemala, I had the privilege of baptising her as she gave testimony to the reality of the Living Christ who speaks and leads today.

Awesome!

The ability to recognize God and to be open to the surprise of his voice comes when we are active worshippers. As we learn to know God, understand his ways and learn to quiet our own voice and the noise in our life – we can then start to hear God.

It's easy to fake 'hearing' God, especially in the climate of expressive worship. Sometimes we make the mistake of thinking that God speaks in only one way and we wrongly assume that those who 'look' the part of a worshipper, are actually worshipping in response to the prompting of God.

I have a friend who is a well-known worship leader. A number of years ago he expressed his frustration at some people who come to worship services and seemingly give their all in a musical expression of worship of Jesus. Everything he observed from the front indicated that these people were enraptured with their Lord and Saviour. Their body language and tears gave evidence to all who observed them that they were in that special, intimate place with the Creator of the Universe. And many envied them for it.

And yet, what frustrated my friend was knowing that even though their Sunday morning worship was elegant and extravagant, their weekday worship was non-existent. One of the people was openly involved in sexual promiscuity. She had been approached by friends and pastoral staff, confronting her with her sin, but she remained belligerently unrepentant.

And so this worship leader looked upon their outward offerings of worship to God in much the same way as God did the people of Israel in Amos' day when he said to the people of Israel:

> *I will not accept your burnt offerings and grain offerings. I won't even notice all your choice peace offerings. Away with your hymns of praise! They are only noise to my ears. I will not listen to your music, no matter how lovely it is. Instead, I want to see a mighty flood of justice, a river of righteous living that will never run dry. (Amos 5:22-24 – NLT)*

Our public worship means nothing if our private lives are out of sync with his desire for holiness and purity. Not that we have to be perfect in order to have our worship accepted. God accepts our imperfection because he covered it and continues to cover it with the blood of Jesus. But we need to know and obey the prompting of the Holy Spirit as he brings things up in and about our lives that need to be addressed, that need to be changed.

The process of worship is simple: us to him, him to us, us to others. We give to God. He speaks to us – affirms us, corrects us, guides us, comforts us. As we give our worship to him he will begin to mould and shape us into his image. And from the overflow of our obedience in obeying his prompting, we spread the fragrance of his presence to others.

Listening to and obeying the Spirit saves our worship from being so personal that it never goes beyond *me*. While knowing and obeying his prompting often begins with me it also invites me to interact with others. Not only does our worship change us, it begins to impact others.

If our worship is only an outward display of expressive response in corporate worship and not easily seen in the way we live our life, we are not hearing God.

True worship opens us up to the needs of others. When we worship in truth and love, we become increasingly aware of his voice in our life – even when there is a lot of noise competing for our attention. When we worship, we begin to understand God's purpose in our lives. We become more and more sensitive to hearing God tell us where we need to change.

I wonder just how different one day in our communities would be if everyone who loved Jesus would wake up and, with all their heart, pray this prayer:

Lord, in my worship of you today in whatever I am doing, help me to allow you to shape me in your image so that I might be an extension of your presence and an encouragement to one other person.

I believe our world would be revolutionized!

While I believe that the need for contemplative worship and inner healing is essential in a worshipper's life, we have to be very careful that we don't remain rooted in that introspection – that focus on *me*. Ultimately, our faith brings us to the place of sacrifice – giving all we are, all we have, all we will be, to serve Jesus.

If we are truly listening to God, we will hear things that apply to our personal life. God will expose the areas that are not pleasing to him. But more than that, as we learn to discern God's voice, even when it surprises us, we will become more and more aware of the needs of those around us.

When Jesus tells his disciples that he is leaving, they are shattered. Jesus has taken them on a journey that blew their understanding of God out of the water. When they came into a new town, people who couldn't hear suddenly were able to hear. A woman who simply brushed the hem of Jesus' clothes was suddenly healed. Ten men with leprosy who had been stigmatized and rejected by their families, friends and communities, were touched by Jesus and healed. A man with a severe demonic oppression that drove him crazy became whole.

But listen to what Jesus says in John 14:12-14:

> *I tell you the truth, anyone who has faith in me will do what I have been doing. He will do even greater things than these, because I am going to the Father. And I will do whatever you ask in my name, so that the Son may bring glory to the Father. You may ask me for anything in my name, and I will do it.*

Jesus changed the communities in which he lived.

What about us?

He told his disciples that whatever we ask in his name he will do. What would happen if our lives were so immersed in the worship of our Lord that we would live with the power of God in our lives? That is God's expectation – that his people on earth would live lives so powerful that the people who knew them would immediately give glory to God because of their lives.

Imagine what our community would be like if we truly lived as worshippers in the power of our God . . .

Those discouraged would go away encouraged.

Those who had sinned would go away forgiven.

Those in broken relationships would find hope for reconciliation.

Those who were sick would be prayed for and begin to find healing.

Those who came burdened would leave
with the weight taken off their shoulders.

Those who came to church to give would go away
also having received.

And unbelievers would go away saying, "God is there!"

Hearing the voice of the Spirit doesn't happen in just one way. God spoke to Elijah in a still, small voice. He spoke to Naaman through a little girl. He spoke to prophets in dreams and visions. He does speak. But we have to know him well enough to recognize his voice.

In John chapter ten, Jesus says five times that his 'sheep' will recognize his voice (John 10:3,4,5,16,27). Part of what we are given as creatures of God is the ability to hear the Creator's voice. Before we ever became believers, we already heard the prompting of his Spirit calling us to the Father's side (John 6:44). As we mature we must be very careful that we keep on hearing God. We cannot depend on our past experiences or knowledge. The acts of worship and listening are active.

As our faith grows, we will learn to hear God more clearly, more often. Gayle sometimes jokes around and says that she wishes God would just send her an email in the morning with the plan for the day and she would just follow the instructions.

That sounds convenient. But I know what would happen. First of all, it's likely that she would just think that it's spam. Secondly, there are times when the task would just seem too hard and it would be pretty tempting not to open the email at all that day. Other times, the message might be so weird that it just wouldn't make sense to consider it.

God is trustworthy and will not lead us down a wrong path. I believe that Jesus taught the disciples and us the importance of knowing the voice of the Holy Spirit. To attempt to live our lives without nurturing a growing desire and ability to hear and respond to the voice of the Holy Spirit is to invite defeat.

There are those who would argue that to attempt to listen to the voice of the Holy Spirit is only to invite the enemy to lead us astray. But that is not what the Bible teaches. In John chapter ten, Jesus specifically says that his sheep *will* follow him because they recognize his voice. In fact, he says that his flock *will not* follow one whose voice they do not recognize. Jesus expects that his sheep, his followers, *will* hear his voice!

It's interesting that we sometimes have more faith that Satan can speak to us and lead us astray than we have faith that the Holy Spirit – whom Jesus sent – can speak to us and lead us in his ways. The Gospel of John records many of the reasons Jesus gave us for the necessity of the indwelling, speaking, prompting Holy Spirit:

He will lead us into all truth. (John 16:13)

He will remind us of what Jesus said. (John 14:26)

*He will help us to know the mind and will of the Father
and do it just as Jesus did. (John 5:19-20; 8:28)*

He will help to keep our worship real! (John 4:23)

*He will raise our awareness of the needs of others and give us the
power to meet those needs. Jesus said that we, also, would be able
to do the things he did – and greater things as well. (John 14:12)*

*He will show others the kingdom of God by demonstrating
his power in us who believe – just like Jesus did. (John 14:12)*

*He will lead us. By speaking to us, his flock
will recognize his voice and follow. (John 10:3-5,16,27)*

A young woman I know knew her pastor well but he had disappointed her. It was perfectly clear to this woman's highly prophetic insight that the pastor was not following in God's way. She saw him as arrogant and proud – unwilling to listen to the voice of the Holy Spirit.

Then, one day, in the stillness of her devotions, she heard God's voice telling her to go and tell this young pastor that she loved him and that she knew that he was chosen by God to lead his people.

Well, she really didn't want to go there! She really wanted to go and tell him he was proud and arrogant and that God would have his way with him. But that wasn't what God asked. Fortunately, God is patient and he spoke to her several times. Finally the prompting was so strong that she had to go. And so she did.

As she prepared for the meeting, Satan spoke words of defeat and discouragement. He continued to taunt her, telling her that really what this pastor needed was rebuke, not love. But God's voice won out.

As she spoke, the anger that she had felt towards him fell away and she realized that it really wasn't her job to discipline and teach this young pastor. God had asked her to go and confirm to him that he was called. That confirmation opened the door in his life for the Holy Spirit to teach him.

God is speaking to us through his Holy Spirit. He wants us to learn to know his voice – to listen and to obey – so that his work can multiply throughout the earth.

Here are a few thoughts and some things to do to help in listening to the Spirit's prompting:

1. Make time in your week to spend time listening for the Spirit's voice. If you have a regular time of reading your Bible and praying, take one day a week where you come before the Lord and instead of reading Scripture, ask the Lord to speak to your heart. It may be a Scripture passage that he reminds you of (a good reason to make a habit of knowing his word). It may be an act of grace or mercy you observed in another person that you sense God encouraging you to respond to. It may be that you just hear his gentle words of affirmation and acceptance.

2. When you worship, individually or corporately, ask the Holy Spirit to open your ears to hear how he might want you to respond to him in your worship and in your relationships with others. He may remind you of an incident that needs to be corrected, forgiven or addressed in some manner. He may direct you to pray for another person – you may even receive some specific area to pray with them about. He may just want you to kneel even though everyone

else is standing, or to lift your hands and dance though no one else is – a true sacrifice of praise!

3. When the Holy Spirit prompts you to do or say something, be willing to obey. In some situations you will be able to obey immediately. But sometimes, in corporate worship, you may need to determine if it would be more appropriate to carry out the Spirit's prompting later so as not to interrupt what God is doing among others. If he reminds you of a relational conflict with someone who is not present at the time, determine to call or see that person as soon as possible following the service so that you might be able to have your worship of Jesus flow over into obedience to him as you reconcile yourself with others. There may be times when the prompting seems a little bit out of the ordinary, but if it does not contradict Scripture, follow through. Trust God to lead you in his love.

4. Be willing to fail.

Most often I don't follow the prompting of the Spirit because I don't want to be wrong – to fail. But we gain a better understanding of the Spirit's voice by testing it through obedience over time – even if we misunderstand at times and get it wrong – than if we ignore it altogether because we fear we might have heard wrong.

Encourage one another with these words given to each of the seven churches in Revelation 2 and 3: "He who has an ear, let him hear what the Spirit says to the churches. . ." (Revelation 2:7, 11, 17, 29; 3:6, 13, 22).

If we confess our sins,
he is faithful and just
and will forgive us our sins
and purify us from all unrighteousness.
1 John 1:9

CHAPTER NINE

CONFESSION

An act of obedient worship

In the Jewish temple, young priests trembled when they thought about their turn to go into the holy of holies. They had heard stories of what happened when a priest entered without purifying himself. In fact, the priest had to tie a cord around his waist when he entered. If he was impure, he would die and the other priests would pull him out by the cord that hung out of the entrance.

Without the blood of Jesus to protect us we cannot come before God. God, by his very nature, cannot accept our sinfulness. The men and women who lived before Christ's sacrificial death and resurrection, had to bring sacrifices to the temple to purify their lives. But even in those days of tangible sacrifices of animals and crops, God expected a humble and repentant heart. He rejected the people's sacrifices when their hearts and their actions did not reflect integrity and purity.

It is impossible – let me stress that again – it is *impossible* to worship when we belligerently hold on to sin in our lives. When we truly worship, our lives begin to reflect the purity of God. It's not an overnight process. And it's not that we need to be perfect *before* we can worship. However, we do need to be moving in God's direction even when we come face to face with the reality of our humanness. Even Paul was frustrated by his humanness. In the letter to the Romans, he ponders the irony of it all – he is constantly doing what he does not want to do, as if his sinful body is waging war against the purity of his heart (Romans 7:18-19).

But Jesus Christ has given us the power to change. When we confess our sins, he is faithful and just and will forgive our sins. As we confess our sins, we change. As we worship, our sins become more apparent. Worship is like putting a dirty white cloth beside a brand new white cloth. When we stand before Jesus, our sin is much clearer to us. And in the light of his majesty, our sin becomes something we desire to rid ourselves of.

Change towards holiness happens when we recognize our sin and then speak it out. When we face God in worship, we must come knowing God's hatred of all sin. To dare to draw near to God with an unclean heart is human arrogance and, put very simply, sin. Yes, God has already forgiven our sin and sees us as clean before him because of Christ Jesus' sacrifice for us. But too often we live as if his grace was worthless and our lives don't reflect God's life-changing grace.

We can choose. Do we live with hearts that have been changed? Or do we simply live with the *appearance* of God's change in us? True worship is worship that dares to confront sin. It dares to confess shortcomings to one another. It dares the vulnerability of weakness. True worship won't allow us to remain the same.

The Scripture invites us to examine ourselves. And, in the event that we are reminded that someone has reason to be in conflict with us, we are to go and make things right with that person (Matthew 5:23-24).

Confession is an act of obedient worship.

You see, we cannot worship without understanding our sinfulness. We cannot change without asking for forgiveness. When we come face to face with our sin, if we desire to be worshippers of God, we have no other choice but to confess.

First of all, confession is part of our relationship with God. When Jesus teaches his disciples to pray, confession is a key and early part of the prayer:

> *Give us our food for today, and forgive us our sins, just as we have forgiven those who have sinned against us. And don't let us yield to temptation, but deliver us from the evil one. (Matthew 6:11-13)*

The second part of confession takes place between those who love God. James writes: "Confess your sins to each other and pray for each other so that you may be healed" (James 5:16).

Confession is worship that frees us.

When we confess our sin – when we 'speak out' our sin to someone we trust, we are freed from the bondage of it. We are freed from the power of its secret. I remember when I was a kid – when I disobeyed my parents, I felt awful. At first there was the simple fear of being punished. But then there was that terrible feeling in my stomach that wouldn't go away. If I ever tried to go to sleep without telling my mom and dad what I had done, I just couldn't settle down. Even if it was way past my bed time, I would get up, in tears, and go confess to them. And every time, even if I was punished, it was as if a huge weight had been lifted. The burden was gone!

Sadly, as we grow older, we become a little less sensitive to that kind of pressure. We become more adept at covering up our sin, ignoring our guilty conscience and putting it out of our mind. Ultimately, the weight of the sin continues to grow and interfere with our relationship with God.

When we 'speak out' our sin, when we actually articulate the sin, we can begin to deal with it. Telling others our shortcomings is very difficult. For one, it's hard to trust people. Almost all of us have had experiences where we have trusted and have been hurt. But the church in worship is a church that practices confession to one another.

For another, no one ever wants to hang out their dirty laundry for others to see, or for that matter, listen to others hanging out theirs. Our pride and sense of individuality attempts to do everything possible to salvage our good image. As Christians, we've learned that a key part of maintaining that image is keeping our sin hidden. But an act of worship that attempts to deny the sin that God wants us to deal with ultimately robs us of its true expression. Without obedient confession our worship quickly becomes nauseating to God. The language used in the Scriptures is strong . . . your impure sacrifices make God want to puke (Mark 7:14-23; Rev. 3:15-17).

Confession is preparatory. Confession opens the door of worship. When we 'come clean', God can speak clearly to us. True worship is much, much more than a good feeling of closeness to God. Sometimes worship is a horrendous force that drags our deep and hidden sin to the surface. Sometimes worship is painful. But at that moment we have the potential to change. Our worship invites the Holy Spirit to reveal those things which he wants to change in us. Only when we come to God in pure worship, confessing our sin and clearing the path to God's voice, can he break down the barriers to growth and maturity.

Confession cuts through the face of pretense. That's a miracle in a world where ultimate makeovers are celebrated. Confession is one of those things that make those who love God, 'salty'. Unlike the world in which we live, those who are true worshippers of the living God live lives that are life-giving, restorative and relational. While competition, self-indulgence and arrogance define the man or woman of the world, God turns that upside down. A worshipper lives a life that displays the living grace and forgiveness of God. Others see that grace extended within the community of faith.

Or they don't.

Godly confession is one of the most difficult things to do in the church. Satan loves to mess with our relationships. He loves to take a trusting relationship and smash it because he knows that if those who love God would live lives of confession, forgiveness and worship it would turn the world upside down. And Satan will do everything in his power to keep that from happening. The tearing down of the old, the corrupt and the rotten makes it possible to build the healthy, the beautiful and the strong.

Imagine if the church were truly a reconciling community! Where people of all ages were free to confess their sins, extend forgiveness and then, in love, restore each other in the name of Jesus. Wow!

Psalm 66:18 says: "If I had cherished sin in my heart, the Lord would not have listened." In worship, God invites us to become more and more like Jesus – to be changed into his likeness. He gives us every opportunity to break the hold sin has on us.

A time of public confession, repentance and intercession can help build the church because others in the worship service recognize God among his people: God touching people's hearts; God healing people's wounds; God breaking people's habitual chains of sin; God helping to make the church, not a place of near perfect specimens of holy ardour, but rather, a place of growth and maturity for real-life people.

The Catholic church still practices the use of the confessional. Confession is freeing. Men, women and children can go to the priest and tell him their sins. They can 'speak out' the things that are wrong and start to work through them. The speaking of our sin is the first step to forgiveness. The Reformation changed that practice. At the time, the ceremony and tradition of the confessional had lost most of its meaning. The revival that happened during the Reformation brought people to their knees, confessing their sins one to another – without the need of the confessional or a priest.

Bu as the church has become more and more comfortable with itself, confession – public and private – has been pushed aside. Some parts of evangelical Christianity have tended to neglect public confession of sin completely, except in the case of a person coming to Christ.

But confessions aren't shared just so that we can feel good about leaving the guilt of a sin behind and then go on living as we did before. Blurting out our sin and then turning around and committing the same sin is not God's plan. Confession is the first step towards changed behaviour. Sometimes change comes slowly, but true confession with a contrite heart leads to change.

Confession is an act of worship. We confess one to another out of reverence for God – so that he might continue to claim more and more of our lives and living – so that he will continue cleansing us and making us holy.

There has been a wealth of literature and self-help material about accountability partners, mentors and spiritual advisors whose primary purpose is to walk alongside believers to help them focus on their spiritual journey. The beauty of these relationships is that they provide for a safe, non-judgmental environment in which to confess our sins to each other and to forgive each other. The mentor or spiritual advisor is there to keep believers accountable and to remind us of choices we've made and the path we've chosen to walk. Mentors and spiritual accountability partners are there when we are in the deepest despair and when our joy can hardly be contained. They are there when we are on a plateau or trudging through a valley. They encourage us, and when necessary, confront us.

I once ministered in a Spanish/English congregation in Archbold, OH. I had been invited to present a Friday and Saturday worship seminar and then to preach on Sunday morning.

As we worshipped Sunday morning God began to work in my heart. First, he brought conviction upon my heart regarding a lie I had told to the pastor and his wife. I had relayed a story to the pastor and his wife Friday afternoon on the way to the church from the airport. On my flight from Toronto, I had been sitting next to a young Jehovah's Witness missionary. We had been in a great discussion but the flight had ended before I had finished saying all that I had intended to say. As I told the story to the pastor and his wife, I embellished it slightly – you know, just to make it a bit better than it really was (evangelastically speaking)! I included the end of the conversation – the part I had intended to say, but just didn't get around to saying.

Then God wanted me to confess it. I knew he was right so I told him that, immediately following the service, I would talk to the pastor and his wife and confess my sin to them. But the Spirit replied, "No, I want you to confess it openly before the congregation before you preach."

I *really* didn't want to go there!

And lastly, as if it wasn't enough that I had to openly spill out my short-comings to a church that not only didn't really know me, but had paid me to come and speak to them, the Holy Spirit told me to preach on a different subject than I had prepared. After all the forethought, preparation and rehearsals of my message I now had to 'fly by the seat of my pants'!

Now flexibility isn't my greatest gift. I like to have everything neatly planned and decided before I go. I hate changing plans mid-stream. But the Holy Spirit clearly indicated that the sermon I had prepared was to be filed and I was to preach on Peter getting out of the boat (Matthew 14).

The worship singing ended and the moderator stood to introduce the guest speaker as, "a man of God who has already blessed us with his teaching and ministry with the worship teams this weekend. What an honour it is to have him here this morning to speak the word of God to us."

Man! Did he have to say that? After an introduction like that how was I to openly confess that this "man of God" was a liar? "Now would be a great time to come back, Jesus!" I did not want to confess that morning. I did not want to speak either. I would have loved to find a hole to crawl into.

But, by the grace of God, I obeyed. It seems that God teaches us humility best through humiliation!

My honesty (and my public humiliation) gave the Holy Sprit a powerful opportunity to challenge and change hearts in the congregation that morning. You see, the Holy Spirit led me in the ways of his truth. He saw through the lie I carelessly spit out and graciously offered me his power to impact this church in a greater way than I could ever have anticipated!

My opening confession gave a context to the message God wanted me to speak. I took a risk. God gave me a powerful message about Peter stepping out of the boat and walking on the water towards Jesus. At the end of the message I felt prompted to invite people to the front who desired to keep taking risks for Jesus. Many people responded. The pastor told me later that about half of the people at the altar were his elders who had been struggling with the direction God seemed to be wanting them to take as a church. Most of them were unwilling to risk stepping out on faith. It was, the pastor said, a message from God specifically for their church.

And God knew the message I had prepared wasn't right for that morning. He knew that the right message for that morning was a demonstration of a humble confession and a call to risk for the sake of his kingdom.

It continues to humble me when I think that my own confession of sin opened the doors for God to speak in that hour. Out of the rubble of a lie God accomplished his purposes. But how much more frightening to think of how many times I miss the opportunity to bring God's personal message to a group of people because I am not listening or my sin is blocking God's voice.

I'm not sure that every church service needs to have a weekly public confession time. In fact, I fear that if it becomes a part of a tradition or a slot that we fill in a service order it will quickly lose its impact. But I know without a doubt that as worshippers we are to invite people to keep short accounts with God and with each other. I know that the power of the church would be multiplied many, many times over if we confessed our sins to one another and cleared the way for God to speak to us. I believe that renewal and restoration can happen, but they will start with confession.

Here are a few things that I have learned about confession:

1. Keep short accounts with God. Don't let sin pile up. When God shows you areas in your life that fall short – deal with them!

2. Find a friend who will walk with you. Ask God to help you find someone you can trust with your heart. This friend should be willing to challenge you and you need to be willing to listen with an open heart.

3. Understand that when your sin impacts others, you have to get to the root of the problem. If you have hurt someone or broken a

relationship, you need to go to that person. Do it face to face, if at all possible. Is it hard? Oh, yes. Our pride gets in the way of admitting that we have failed. But going to that person and asking for their forgiveness is the only way to lift the burden.

4. Challenge your church leadership to include times of confession in your worship services. If you are a leader in your congregation, listen to God's voice as you speak. God does not always do things in expected ways.

When I was a youth pastor in my mid-thirties, I stood in front of the congregation ready to preach my sermon. Suddenly, the weight of Christ's overwhelming love in the midst of our preoccupation and unconfessed sin was so great that when I opened my mouth to speak all that came out was sobs. For fifteen minutes (while Gayle was slowly dying in the pews) I wept. But that wordless sermon moved the hearts of the men and women that God wanted to speak to that morning.

5. Join a small group of people who are committed to growing together, learning together and caring enough for each other to be willing to be open with each other – willing to confess your sins one to another and thereby receive the forgiveness and healing from the Lord.

6. Always obey the slightest prompting of the Holy Spirit.

How beautiful on the mountains are the feet of those who bring good news,
who proclaim peace, who bring good tidings, who proclaim salvation,
who say to Zion, "Your God reigns!"
Isaiah 52:7

CHAPTER TEN

PROCLAIMING
Advertising the things that God is doing

The stories in the Bible take on a near mythical value. Sometimes we lose the reality of our God – a God that can change our lives in dynamic ways – a God that can make the blind see and the deaf hear, the lame to walk and the sick healthy again. Do we merely understand the stories intellectually, or are we experiencing them in our daily lives?

The word 'proclaim' means to make bold and public statements. We can also use words like announce, shout, declare, boast, advertise and publish. Walking in worship means that we will boldly proclaim, announce, shout, declare, boast, advertise and publish the things that God is doing in our life, in our friends' lives, in our community and in our world.

We all understand what it means to advertise. Companies advertise their products so that people will know to buy them. We know that people buy products they feel comfortable with. If we see a product on TV, in magazines and on billboards, we feel confident to purchase it.

To publish is equally familiar. We publish something that we want other people to know about. When someone is engaged or receives a promotion or celebrates a fiftieth anniversary, we publish it. We publish biographies of people who have impacted our society.

As worshippers, we are to advertise – to publish the works, activities and characteristics of God – the things he is doing in our lives and in our world. We proclaim God's attributes. We announce God's activities. We declare God's names. We publish God's qualities.

By telling others about the acts and attributes of God I engage my awareness of God – right now – in the real world. While I pray that God would continue impacting my life in such dynamic ways that I won't have to look so hard to recognize his activity each and every day, I do need practice watching for it. By telling others how the power of God is active in my life, I am forced to watch for God. When I recognize the things that God is doing in me and around me, I can't help but tell others. More than that, I will worship – because God has shown himself to be greater than my human capacity. In many ways, I cannot even understand God, even though I can articulate his attributes. God is far greater than I can speak. But as I learn to speak ofjust a fragment of his grace and goodness, I am bound to worship in more meaningful ways.

Second, telling the story of what God is doing in our lives, especially in settings where God's people meet, helps to encourage others to tell their stories as well. While the word 'sharing' has the connotation of campfires and testimony meetings, we need to get past the old baggage and begin again to talk about what God is doing in our lives. Too often we only use

Scripture or other people's stories to tell of the goodness of God. When we walk in worship and live 'in step' with God, he will do great things in our lives. As we publish the acts of God, we invite others to rejoice with us. More than that, we help others look for God's activity in their own lives. If we have no story to tell, no need to shout out and proclaim the acts of God, then we are not walking in relationship with God.

Third, proclamation of the things of God invites the curious and the seekers to look further. As those who worship God tell of his goodness, those looking for God will come to discover the mysteries that we have found. In every revival, word spread like wildfire. People were drawn to those who loved God because they found something there that was impossible to find anywhere else.

When we announce the things that God is doing, we point the way for seekers to find God. We are living in a time when seeking some sort of spiritual experience or expression of spirituality is at an all time high. People are not only looking for answers in science or in education, they are seeking out spiritual sources. Witches, seers, alternative religions and new-age spiritualism are flourishing. Are they missing an encounter with the one true God because believers have stopped looking for and proclaiming his greatness?

Several things happen when we proclaim God:

Our worship shows us who our God is, what he is like, what he has done, what he is doing and what he has promised he will do.

Those who love God become closer together and are able to act as a unified force, led by a common vision.

The curious and those who are looking for some spiritual connection with God begin to desire to know the God we boast about.

Our proclamation reveals our understanding of God. When we tell others in our community that God is the one who provides for us, we are forced to consciously identify the ways that God *is* acting in our lives. We become more cognizant of God's activity and power in our *lives*, not just our own skill, background or sheer luck.

When we tell others of the way that God leads us, we look to him for leadership in real ways. We understand how much more we need to hear his voice and follow him (John 10:1-30). As we start to recognize the ways that God *has* led – even if they are just small examples – we begin to believe that God *will* lead and we follow that leadership with a new passion.

When we announce God as able to win the battles we are fighting, we begin to trust him to fight for us in all circumstances. As we take baby steps of trust, we start to call out to God no matter what the challenges that face us. Identifying the ways that God is taking hold of impossible situations builds our confidence in his ability and willingness to fight on our behalf.

When we meditate on God and begin to understand him as a judge who judges all things in righteousness, we begin to see our own sinfulness. Contemplating the purity of God clarifies our understanding that we cannot hide from his holy presence. God will judge out of his holiness. He will deal with each person justly. But as we grow in our worship, we will also see that God tempers his judgement with mercy. Yes, his judgement is just – but he will rule with grace and mercy.

Our expressions of God as our Redeemer and Saviour, the One who extends mercy and salvation to us, focuses our attention on our own need for renewal. We crave the mercies of God each and every day. Our dependence is on God and the power of his Spirit, not on our own discipline as we struggle to live holy lives. We respond with gratitude and wonder that we should have received so great a salvation.

When we recognize God as our 'Abba' or 'Daddy', the most intimate name for a father, we catch a fragment of what it means to be a child in the family of God. Acknowledging God as our Father allows us to rest in his love, tenderness and care. But more than that, we yearn for his instruction, correction and guidance, like a father in whom we have complete confidence.

As the body of Christ, our worship declares our unity in the understanding of all we know God to be. We need to tell the stories of how God has changed us. That is really what proclamation means.

After God brought the Israelites out of Egypt, he prompted the people to celebrate the Passover. This was not a nebulous Jewish holiday. The Passover was a time when the people proclaimed that God was faithful and that his power saved the entire nation.

We need to celebrate the things that God has done in our lives. As a part of our corporate worship, we need to tell the stories of the miracles of God. When we tell of the power of God, we build the body. Telling the story helps others in our community look for God's interaction and provision in new ways.

We all hear stories of God's miraculous intervention in the lives of super-spiritual people. Several years ago, many women across Canada immersed themselves in a book that talked about what happened when women prayed. Many became discouraged because their own lives did not reflect the miracles the book talked about. But I wonder if what really happened was that the real stories of the prayers (and answers to the prayers) of ordinary people remained untold. We get so caught up in our lives that we forget that, even in the little things, God is there. We need to tell the stories of how God, in small and yet powerful ways, has impacted our day-to-day lives.

True worship draws us into the depths of intimacy and to the heights of extravagant praise. True worship helps us to see the power of God – even in the ordinary. True worshippers openly proclaim the work of God in their lives. Open proclamation is an expression of unity by the body of Christ. It is what really distinguishes the followers of Jesus.

Sometimes we miss the power of God in the sheer simplicity of it. In a ridiculously simple yet unfathomably complex statement, Jesus tells us that the world around us will know we are his followers when they see how much we love each other (John 13:35). Our acts of love, because of the work of Jesus, express and proclaim all of who God is – clearly and purposefully. Our love shouts out the character of God to those that watch.

When the body of Christ proclaims their worship of God publicly, another thing happens – their worship invites those who are searching for answers to come and meet Jesus. Our lives, our love, our trust, our words compel them to come to us; to our homes, to the places we work and play, and to our church to find out what is behind the expressions of worship they see in us.

We live in a fast-paced, technology-centred culture. We are clever. We have access to almost unlimited information, we are self-satisfied and self-indulgent. The church and Christians as a whole are suspect. They are seen as small minded, a little bit simple to believe in God, especially in a world that has 'proof' that God has indeed ceased to exist. Perhaps we have let God die. Perhaps, because we don't proclaim our God – because we don't 'advertise' his activities – our society cannot see God at work. Perhaps we have been silent so long that we no longer see God as a dynamic and engaging God.

I teach in many Discipleship Schools across North America. I am struck by how many of the students I meet are surprised to hear that God acts in miraculous ways. They have heard Bible stories and missionary stories, but they have not heard their parents, their teachers, or their ministers tell the stories of how God has moved in their lives in this generation. They are shocked when they hear men and women of God tell their stories of how God has changed their lives and impacted their communities. If our children cannot see a powerful God, is it any wonder that the world sees God as passé?

If we, who say we believe in the living, active, very present God, don't see his imprint in our world and therefore can't declare what we see, is it any wonder the people who have never met Jesus don't recognize the things he does?

Proclaiming our love for God publicly is worship. Openly announcing the acts and attributes of God can be done in many different ways. God will prompt each community in the ways that will best suit that community. It may be a concert in the park or the revival of the coffee-house. It may be going to the places where people in the community live and play and simply getting to know them on a persoanl basis. It may be starting a youth program, a health centre, a social services clinic, ESL classes, basic car-care courses . . . the possibilities are limitless.

But I know that however God asks you to proclaim his name, it will start with how we live our lives, how we tell our stories, what we say when great things happen to us, how we react when trouble comes, what we do about the needs we see around us, how we treat each other. If God is truly the One who knows us by name and loves the very essence of who we are; if God is a powerful Healer who cures sickness; if God truly is able to make broken hearts whole and set free those taken captive by sin, then we need to shout it out to our community. As his followers we are living testaments, living witnesses, to him who lives in us.

It sounds so simple, doesn't it? It's as easy as our desire to bring those we care about to God. But there are many barriers. When our oldest son was about four years old he asked his uncle if he loved Jesus. My first reaction was to stop his question and carefully explain that we need to be cautious about how we approach others and how we speak about God with them.

Can you believe it?

But we are cautious about how we speak of Jesus. We are cautious about offering to pray for a co-worker who is struggling. We may say a passing, "I'll pray for you," but do we dare to take a moment out of our day to sit with them and pray for them right there? When something in our job goes really right, are we willing to give the credit to God? How willing are we to humble ourselves in a situation where we were wrong and ask a co-worker to forgive us?

Jesus said that we are to be the kind of people that bring salt to our world (Mark 9:50). Our job is to make the world taste better! Yet the Christian is almost always portrayed as weak, proud or out of touch. Perhaps we have not been telling the story of our great and good God. Perhaps we have been so afraid that God would not pull through that we kept quiet. But our lives and our words are to proclaim the lordship of Jesus in our lives.

Christianity that has no impact on society is not how Jesus imagined it. Worship of Jesus that is never seen in public is restricting at best, self-serving at worst. If we believe what we say in our songs, in our prayers and in our sermons, then we cannot keep worship of God from breaking out of our worship groups, our churches. We cannot be the silent in the land. To hold our worship of God so tightly to ourselves that its life never spills out onto the streets is to ignore what Jesus said in Matthew 5:14-16:

You are the light of the world – like a city on a mountain, glowing in the night for all to see. Don't hide your light under a basket. Instead, put it on a stand and let it shine for all. In the same way, let your good deeds shine out for all to see, so that everyone will praise your heavenly Father. (NLT)

Our world desperately needs a God who saves. They need to see a light shining brightly in the midst of encroaching darkness. They need a standard against which to measure the effects of the darkness upon them and society at large. But they will only see their need of a Saviour as they hear and see him proclaimed through us. Our God *has* done mighty things! He *has* demonstrated his power in the past and today. He *has* given us the Holy Spirit that we might be the hands and feet of Jesus upon the earth today. And he *has* commanded that we should announce his activity among the nations:

> *With joy you will drink deeply from the fountain of salvation! In that wonderful day you will sing: 'Thank the LORD! Praise his name!' Tell the world what he has done. Oh, how mighty he is! Sing to the LORD, for he has done wonderful things. Make known his praise around the world. (Isaiah 12:3-5 – NLT)*

We regularly have Jehovah's Witnesses coming to our door. They know that I am a pastor. I never slam the door in their faces. In fact, I rather enjoy speaking with them. A few years ago I spent three months in Guatemala to learn Spanish. During the last six weeks of my stay I lived in a home belonging to a woman who had suffered immensely through an abusive husband. The Jehovah's Witnesses reached out to her and helped her to start her life over again.

We had many conversations about what we believed. Having had many students in her home over the past 15 years (her only source of income) she had learned the graciousness of listening to the beliefs of others and finding areas of convergence with what she believed. When I spoke to her about my Anabaptist beliefs she was excited to find that we both shared a peace theology. When she learned of our history of sharing our resources with the needy at home and around the world, she again rejoiced at that area of agreement with what she also believed.

I learned much about Jehovah's Witness theology and practice because of her joy in speaking about it with me. And she learned much about my own theological perspectives of Jesus as I spoke to her of my relationship with him. I told her the Jesus of the New Testament is the same Jesus today. I told her of the things that I had experienced and how his church, even today, sees miracles happen.

Jehovah's Witness theology isn't big on the miraculous works of Christ still being accomplished through his people today. But I spoke to my Guatemalan mom about Heather, a teenager on a mission trip to Mexico with her youth group. I was involved in a five day training program with about 200 young people preparing to spend two weeks sharing their faith in Jesus Christ with the Mexican people. One of the training events was to put on a fiesta in one of the poorer neighbourhoods. Heather was over six feet tall and strong. She loved to laugh and joke around and play with the kids. Her joy and love for the kids was very much a valuable asset to her team. Heather and her youth group were about to present a drama toward the end of our time at the fiesta when she had an accident.

While crossing the lawn she stepped into a hole covered over by the grass. Her leg went into the hole about half-way to her knee. Her height, weight and momentum kept her moving forward. The friend walking with her heard a sickening crack. Heather fell down in severe pain. Only a few meters away, Scott, her youth pastor, heard her cry out and rushed over. As they pulled her leg from the hole, the youth pastor and others on the team saw and felt the bones in the leg moving as if there was another joint between the knee and the ankle.

A couple of the youth were sent to get me and find out what they should do next. When I reached Heather, her leg was terribly swollen and she was in significant pain. Before sending them off to the hospital, we paused to pray. As I prayed, I felt this anger rising in me against what the enemy had done to this young servant of God. In my brief prayer, I declared that Satan had no jurisdiction in this girl's life. I boldly proclaimed the authority of Christ, given to all who believe, and declared that what the enemy had done would be made null and void – that Jesus would restore to Heather the use of her leg as if it had never happened.

The team then loaded up the van and headed off to the hospital. Three hours later, the team returned to the campus and Heather got out of the van walking! She said that the x-ray had shown that her leg had *never been broken*! She had told the doctor that it indeed *had* been broken but that Jesus had healed it. The doctor tried to convince her that, because of her great pain, she probably had just imagined that she felt the bone breaking and saw it moving. But that didn't explain why her friends also saw the bones move or why her youth pastor saw and felt the bones moving around when he held her leg in his hands when they transported her into a shady area. The movement was significant enough that his concern was that the broken bones not dislocate and come punching out through the skin. No, in spite of the doctor's unbelief, they all knew and believed that they had experienced the miraculous intervention of the power of God.

When my Guatemalan house-mom heard the story of Heather, she was amazed! She had never heard of God doing those things today – at least not from someone who had witnessed it firsthand. Declaring the works of God made an impression on her. I believe it will bring about new perspectives in her life of wanting to know and live for Jesus – a Jesus that she has only heard parts about through her Jehovah's Witness theology.

When we proclaim God's attributes and activity as we experience them, we challenge others to look beyond their own existence and discover the many ways in which God wants to make himself known. We give worship to God through our declaration and invite others to be more attentive to God and what he is doing in their lives and in the community surrounding them. In essence, we invite them to join us in worship.

We need to start taking small steps to telling the stories of how God is working in our lives. Here are a few ways that I am working on to help my worship walk intersect with my life:

1. Learn who God is.

   I try to study the Bible and find out all the different ways his people understood him. The Jewish people rarely used the name 'God', but rather used names that described God's attributes. I've found that a good Bible dictionary helps me to get a handle on the meaning of the names of God. Gayle is now challenging me to re-language the names I've learned, replacing the 'churchy' words for words I would normally use. As I learn more names and attributes of God I try to link those to real life. The hardest part is to work on being specific and personal in recognizing God. Too often I find myself simply accepting the good things that God does as normal or ordinary. But as I practice telling the story of God in my life, I am always surprised at just how much God is doing.

2. Try to remember how God has revealed himself to you.

   When I worship in private times, I tell God how I see him in my own life. Things like; "Lord you are gentle and compassionate, slow to anger, overflowing with love. I have experienced your gentle hand of comfort for me this week as I struggle with the death of my father. Thank you!"

3. When you are worshipping in public (preaching, reading, singing, or sharing), try to take note of the words that reveal God's character. Meditate on them later.

Sometimes I am seduced by the beauty of the music and the harmonies and I forget the words. I have tried to take the words out of the music on occasion and look at them as poetry, concentrating on how the words alone express God's attributes.

4. Simply ask God to give you the mind of Christ.

I try to pray that the Holy Spirit would show me how to demonstrate his presence to those I meet during the day. It's easier to talk about God when I am in teaching assignments – after all, that is what I am there for. But I am trying to learn to speak of God in my daily life, to my neighbours and people I meet in my community. I pray that God would give me the boldness to obey when he asks me to speak.

5. Consciously look for ways to be a Godly encouragement to someone each day. We really don't have to use 'spiritual words' or 'Christianized words' in order to proclaim God's attributes, activities and character. We just have to be willing to be used in simple ways. Trust God to open the doors. He will have already prepared the way for the person to be encouraged by what you have to say as you advertise, publish, announce, shout, declare and boast about his activities today.

The heavens declare the glory of God;
the skies proclaim the work of his hands.
Day after day they pour forth speech;
night after night they display knowledge.
Psalm 19:1-2

CHAPTER ELEVEN

KNOWING HIS CREATION
Recognizing his image

The psalmist was attuned to the heart-stirring beauty of God's creation! He saw God's awesome power in the skies. He didn't hesitate to sing, talk and tell others about the wonders he saw in the natural world.

I know most of us live in a world of concrete and asphalt. Multiply that by the speed at which we live, we don't often take time to enjoy the world God created. God's creation is awesome! In the spring I think about God's plan to rejuvenate and revive. As a Canadian, I can't help but think about God's life-giving power in spring. When I see a tiny purple crocus struggling out of the near frozen ground – often still partially covered with snow – I know that God has the power to give life. For several springs, a family of robins came to nest in our front porch. The nest design was intricate and strong enough to last the season. The diligence and care the parents gave their infants was fascinating.

God shows his power, creativity and majesty in creation. The stars in their sheer numbers and distance display the majesty of God. When we study the solar system we cannot help but praise a God who planned such a complex system.

If you have ever watched an approaching storm over the prairies, you know the frightening power of God. I grew up on a farm. Dark clouds in the west, the rising winds, cool air competing with hot humidity only meant one thing – God was preparing to give his people a show that would mesmerize. I have heard the frightening roar of distant thunder and watched spectacular lightening. I have seen entire crops destroyed in a matter of minutes by God's hand and at other times, nurtured by a gentle three day rain. God is powerful.

God has unlimited creativity in his creation. I have had the opportunity to travel in many parts of Canada, the United States, Mexico, Central and South America, England and Ireland. I never tire of God's creation. Each place has its own sense of beauty and wonder. I remember when I first saw the Rocky Mountains of western Canada. No picture can describe the awesome feeling of looking up the sheer cliffs. No one prepared me for the surprising beauty of the mountains in the spring when the run-off from the melting snow feeds thousands of tiny mountain flowers boasting their beauty on the mountain side. Their blossoms only last a few weeks, but the cliffs are spectacular for those few weeks. The sound of waterfalls cutting through the rock, their power slowly eating away at the solid rock until deep crevices scar the mountain, never fails to amaze me.

I grew up on the prairies of southern Manitoba and still long for the breadth of vision that the wide open fields offer. The open plain is so vast that you are able to see the horizon rise in the distance. As the early morning dew evaporates, a shimmering mirage creates mysterious visions on the horizon. The grains, the wind, the heat, the cold – all of these contrasts make the prairies uniquely beautiful.

One of the most dynamic experiences I've had was standing on the top of Pacaya, a volcanic mountain in Guatemala, and feeling the tremendous heat generated by the hot lava inside the volcanic crater. As I stood at the crater's edge, I could see in the distance volcano Fuego spitting sulphuric blasts into the sky. Just watching that spectacular view, knowing I was standing at the crater's edge of an active volcano that could erupt at any moment, made me tremble at the powerful unpredictability of creation.

I have been drenched by the consistent sheets of wispy drizzle in the rainforest, celebrated the gentle breezes in the enveloping humidity and witnessed the colourful mosaic of autumn among the rolling hills. I've listened to the constant rhythm of the ocean waves, felt the crisp chill of the morning air as the snow crunched like fresh stretched leather beneath my feet.

Our God has an imagination! A wonderful, creative, surprising imagination. Our Creator has made a world of diversity. Two rivers, yes! But oh, so amazingly dissimilar from each other! Two mountain ranges, yes! But no tree or crevice upon it alike. Two sunsets, yes! But no hue the same.

God's creativity is incredible! As I stop, just for a moment, and look at God's creation, I am in awe of his incredible gifts of pleasure to us. And I worship. His creation continually calls us to praise him.

Often, as I look and watch and celebrate, I hear the words Brian Doerksen wrote in a modern-day psalm that beautifully captures a part of this almost involuntary response to praise the almighty creator when faced with the awesomeness of his masterpieces.

CREATION CALLS

I have felt the wind blow, whispering Your name
I have seen Your tears fall when I watch the rain

How could I say there is no God
When all around creation calls
A singing bird, a mighty tree
The vast expanse of open sea

Gazing at a bird in flight, soaring through the air
Lying down beneath the stars, I feel Your presence there

I love to stand at ocean's shore
And feel the thund'ring breakers roar
To walk through golden fields of grain
`neath endless blue horizon's frame

Listening to a river run, watering the earth
The fragrance of a rose in bloom, a newborn's cry at birth

I believe. I believe. I believe

Water flowing over the edge of a precipice
Turning misty white as it falls into the pool below

Tall evergreens, at the river's edge, standing on guard
While a deer and fawn drink from the stream

The smell of tilled earth, just after the rain
A rainbow, dazzling natural colours

The sight of a hawk as it circles in the thermal drafts of summer
A flock of Canada geese flying in perfect formation

Rising from the valley floor, rolling hills covered with trees
Birch, maple, elm, beech turning fiery red, yellow and gold in the autumn air

A leaf on its brief journey, twisting, turning, dancing its way to the ground
Lifting our eyes, the mountains rise, trees giving way

Giving way to rock, cliffs, ice, glaciers and majestic jagged peaks
As the sun slips behind the horizon and night falls,

The mountains become silent fortresses silhouetted against the night sky
The countless stars shining in silent testimony

Snowflakes, gently falling, falling each unique, whispering
'Remember the mercy of God . . . remember the mercy . . .'

Covering all the world in white and then
The quiet, quiet, quiet of creation at rest.

1994 Mercy/Vineyard Publishing (Brian Doerksen)

God's creation reinforces our belief in a creator, in a God who is much more than an idea or ideology. This glorious world did not happen by chance.

But there's more . . .

To know God's creation is not only to recognize his image in the things he created but to recognize him in the people he has created. We are made in God's image. That means that each of us carries echoes of God in us. Christian and non-Christian alike are made in the image of God. To look into the eyes of another person is to recognize the image of God even when that image is only a fragment or a glimmer.

Sometimes that image is scarred and damaged. Sometimes we have to look deep into the core of the person to find the tiny bits of God's image that remain.

Do we recognize the image of God in the people we meet? Seeing God in the people we meet means that we treat them with the respect that they deserve. We look past the things that are ugly and damaged and begin to see in them the perfect image of God. We understand that at the core of all people, there is a God who made them in his image.

Sometimes our own expectations of how the package *should* look destroys our ability to see the tenderness inside. God looks past the piercings, the metal, the spikes, the scars, the foul language, and sees the heart. And so should we.

As I look through Scripture from Genesis through Revelation I see a God who created all people – even though many of those people turned their backs on him. I see a God of compassion who not only calls a people group (the Jews) to be his people but extends that call to all those who seek his face. I see a God who yearns to have his people draw near so he can gather them up in his arms (Ezekiel 20:34) and brood over them like a mother hen (Luke 13:34).

Then God said, 'Let us make man in our image, in our likeness, and
let them rule over the fish of the sea and the birds of the air, over the
livestock, over all the earth, and over all the creatures that move
along the ground.' So God created man in his own image, in the
image of God he created him; male and female he created them.
(Genesis 1:26-27)

After seeing all that he had made in the natural world God noticed that it
was good. But he needed one more creation. God's creative design of his
worshippers, you and me, was to make us in his own image: people who
would reflect the Creator; people with the capacity to rule as God ruled;
people with the ability to choose as God chose; people with the
imagination to create similarly as God created. And God looked at his
creation and decided it was very good!

We all know the story – creation didn't stay in the perfection of sinless-
ness. We all have fallen short of the possibilities created within us.
However, we remain a people made in the image of God. We have everything we need to be intimate with God if we would accept his free gift of
salvation through the death and resurrection of Jesus and by the power of
his Holy Spirit. Although we might not be empowered by that Spirit or
obedient to Jesus or recognize the name of God, we still bear his image.

And in this created body is his invitation to worship.

Wow! Imagine . . . a personal invitation to worship our Creator! The truly
amazing aspect of being created in God's image is we can move away from
our own selfishness and petty critiques of others and understand that
everyone, even those who are hard to love, hard to live with – *everyone* – is
created in God's image. We are freed to love others as he loves them, not
because they are righteous or even loveable, but because they are created in
the very image of God – a God who loves them and died for them – just like
he loves us and died for us!

Sometimes our worship of God can be something no less profound than simply loving our neighbours as we love ourselves. We are able to see value in people – not because of what they do – but because of whose image we recognize in them. It's hard to love people who are seen to be wicked, immoral, godless, drunken, ugly, unless we can see beyond their sin and outward condition and are able to see the fragments of the creator-God whose image they mirror.

Hebrews 13:2-3 reminds us that angels sometimes disguise themselves as people in need. What an opportunity to bless God through ministering to those who are in need. What an opportunity to worship God through blessing those he has created.

> *Do not forget to entertain strangers, for by so doing some people have entertained angels without knowing it. Remember those in prison as if you were their fellow prisoners, and those who are mistreated as if you yourselves were suffering. (Hebrews 13:2-3)*

When I was a youth pastor, each September we would go to all the school grounds the youth in our group attended and pray. We would pray for their Christian friends in the school. We would pray for the students and teachers of each school. We would pray for the administrators and parents. I would also ask the students to list the names of teachers whom they respected for how they cared for them as students in their classes. One of the students gave a couple of names but then replied, "But they aren't Christians." I responded saying that because people are all made in the image of God anytime they do those things which agree with image of their Creator they reflect him to others – even if they themselves are not believers.

When we see the image of God reflected in others and thank God for those reflections – we worship. When we refuse to give in to prejudice and judgment and serve the needy, we worship. When we can look past the outward imperfections and recognize the image of Jesus – we worship.

I am not really a student of nature. But sometimes when I go for walks, I get caught up in my own thoughts and ideas and miss much of what God is showing around me or saying to me. Sometimes I need the spectacle of lightening and thunder to jar me awake to God's creation.

I am also not naturally inclined to see all of the people I meet as creatures made in the image of God. Sometimes the damage of the world is so great that I only see the scars. But as I learn to worship, I begin to understand the importance of seeing the image of God reflected in others. I begin to respond with thankfulness to God for those reflections of all he intended. And I pray for his purposes and intentions to be fulfilled in them. As I learn what it means to look after the 'least of these' (Matthew 25:40) – I worship. My worship needs to reflect an understanding of God – seeing the hand of a creator God in all of creation.

I have tried to look for God in a more deliberate way, celebrating his goodness through the world he created. Here are a few things I have tried:

1. Take a walk.

When I walk, I ask God to open my eyes to see – really see – his creation. My dog helps! His fine tuned ears and nose notice things that I often miss. I try to look for evidence of God's presence – even times when I'm playing. I take photos, because that forces me look harder and see the tiny nuances of the different scenes. I look for what he is doing in his creation – and am delighted at God's surprises.

2. Try to think beyond your own definition of 'Christian' or 'good'.

I purposely try to get to know people who don't fit in my little box. I simply tell myself, "God made this person – in his image." And then I ask God to give me his eyes to see them as he does. Then I pray that God will give me the grace that others would see the love of God through me. I want to see each person I meet at their core, the core that still holds the image of God. Yeah, some of the people I meet have really messed with God's image – I've messed with God's image – but I know that at the centre of each person I meet is God's image. I know that he wants me to find that core.

3. Pray for God to give you joy as you try to live with the understanding that you, too, were made in his image.

It's so easy to get caught up in the many imperfections of my own life. Yes, I know I was created in God's image – but I grew up in a strong Mennonite home. Pride was despised. But I struggle with the difference between ungodly pride and ungodly self-abasement. I am created in the image of God. In that image I hold possibilities that I never imagined. Self-debasement or false humility does not celebrate God's image. I fail time and time again to live as a child created in the image of God, but I have an advocate and helper – Jesus and the Holy Spirit are there to help me reflect God in the choices I make.

4. Try to live out the understanding that everyone is made in God's image. Practice it with the people you work or go to school with.

I try to speak and illustrate my understanding of being created in the image of God to the people I interact with. I work at showing each person respect. I try to have the patience to listen to their needs and meet those needs, as I am able. I try to avoid judging them.

5. Remember that there is a world beyond the small world you see. Sometimes the stranger who visits your home or the one you meet on an airplane or reach out to on a street may be an angel!

How can a young person keep their way pure?
By living according to your word.
I seek you with all my heart; do not let me stray from your commands.
I have hidden your word in my heart that I might not sin against you.
Psalm 119:9-11

CHAPTER TWELVE

KNOWING THE WORD

And the Word who became human

While I wonder if it may be ludicrous to write this, I will – knowing God's written word is an important part of being a worshipper of him.

The Scriptures are the word of God. They help guide us, lead us into truth and confirm our relationship with God. Worshippers are those who know his word: who meditate on his promises; who live out his precepts; who retell the stories of the wonders of our God.

The miracle of the Scriptures is that the words are life-giving. The words written generations ago still apply today. Stories recorded more than 2,000 years ago still have a poignant wisdom for today. The word is living, real and powerful.

I have learned hundreds – perhaps even thousands – of new songs over the years and I'm amazed at how many songs come to mind as I am reading Scripture. Many of those songs are not only rooted in the word of God but grow out of significant interaction with a portion of Scripture. God uses these songs to implant his written word in my heart as I sing them. I can meditate upon his word as I sing a passage of Scripture back to him.

While music can help affirm and reaffirm our knowledge of God through his word, we need to know his word for more than just being able to have a great list of Scriptural songs. In the New International Version Bible, Psalm 119 has 24 references to 'your word' (35 in the King James Version Bible). The psalmist begins the section with verse nine asking how a young person can keep their way pure. He responds with the affirmation that purity comes by living according to God's word; seeking him with all their heart; requesting that God not let them stray from his commands. But the action part of these verses is the declaration that worshippers hide God's word in their heart so that they might not sin against him.

Knowing God's word helps us in worship. His word reminds us of who we are and who God is. It reminds us of who we are being called to be – to be like Jesus. It encourages us on the path of purity and intimacy. It acts as our guide – agreeing with what God, by his Holy Spirit, speaks to us.

Hebrews 4:12 says: "The word of God is living and active. Sharper than any double-edged sword, it penetrates even to dividing soul and spirit, joints and marrow; it judges the thoughts and attitudes of the heart."

The word of God is situated at the apex of the joining of life and worship. Our worship is not just repeating words back to God, but taking the words he gives us and meditating on them until they *become* our life. When the word of God lives in us, we are built up.

There are times when God asks me to do things that are way outside the little paradigm I am comfortable with. In those times, I think of Peter and the water incident. Jesus asked Peter to come out and meet him. To do that, he had to step out of the boat and walk on the water. There was no logic to that request. Peter knew that he couldn't walk on water. Yet he stepped out of the boat and *walked on the water* toward Jesus! And then he took his eyes off of Jesus and sank like a rock! But Jesus was there for him. As he was sinking, Jesus stretched out his hand and rescued him, chiding him for his lack of faith (Matthew 14:22-33).

I remember what the author of Hebrews said to his readers about faith – that faith "is the confident assurance that what we hope for is going to happen. It is the evidence of things we cannot yet see" (Hebrews 11:1 – NLT). When God puts me in impossible situations, those words encourage me to step out.

The passages in which Jesus or Paul or John tell us about the frightening events of the future reaffirm one thing – God is in control. When our world seems out of control, the word of God comes to mind and comforts us. God is and will always be in control, even when we can't see any evidence of it.

The way we live our life is to be guided by the prompting of the Holy Spirit in agreement with Scripture. Our worship of God is reflected in our obedience to him. Knowing God's word helps us to better understand the Spirit's urging to perfect in us the image of Christ Jesus.

Memorizing Scripture is a practical way to worship God. Deuteronomy 30:14 says, "The word is very near you; it is in your mouth and in your heart so you may obey it." When we memorize Scripture we dig a deep resource well from which we can draw insight for living as worshippers of God – a measuring stick by which we can confirm the truth of the Spirit's prompting. We also are able to recognize when God brings up aspects of his word in our worship so that he can lead us into greater obedience.

But worship is more than that moment we recognize God. Worship is the moment where our understanding of God becomes evidenced in the way we live our life. The true worshipper is not seeking simply to obey, they are seeking to breathe and live God – to walk out their worship daily. The worshipper who consumes God's word and feeds on Scripture builds a foundation that they can rely on in any situation. The Scriptures provide the foundation of life learning.

The word of God and its influence on our life is much broader than a keen understanding or simple repetition of mere words. In one aspect of worship, we can reaffirm God's word in the music we sing. When we write praises to God or choose songs for worship, our knowledge of God's word should inform and guide us. The song, God's word rephrased and put to music, reminds us again of the truth.

Yet how easily we find comfort in the simple words and the music and only see the song – and miss the Saviour. I often find myself basking in old experiences of God when I worship. The song *How Great Thou Art* reminds me of times that I walked in nature and saw the majestic greatness of God. But I can't stay there. I have to consistently wake up to the words and see God anew and afresh today.

Sometimes as I lead worship, I ask people to step outside of the pleasant melody and familiar words. We can get caught up in the song itself and miss seeing Jesus. As a worship leader, I want to do more than simply entertain people or give people a good feeling. I want to lead them to a place where they can engage in God and bring the words that were written for them into their life. Sometimes I startle the worshippers by stopping at the end of the song *Shout to the Lord* (by Darlene Zschech) and draw people's attention to the last line: "Nothing compares to the promise I have in you." I ask them to reflect, "What are the promises that God has given that make us shout to the Lord?" God's promises are awesome and we do well to consider them as we sing the song:

Never will I leave you; never will I forsake you. (Hebrews 13:5)

I go and prepare a place for you, I will come back and take you to be with me that you also may be where I am. (John 14:3)

'For I know the plans I have for you,' declares the LORD, 'plans to prosper you and not to harm you, plans to give you hope and a future.' (Jeremiah 29:11)

The one who is in you is greater than the one who is in the world. (1 John 4:4)

Nothing will be able to separate us from the love of God that is in Christ Jesus our Lord. (Romans 8:38-39)

WOW! If I can get even a fragment of those promises and really believe them, it will change the way I live my life. Just think about it. God will never leave you, he will never forsake you. Imagine what that means to a mother who has just lost a child? To a spouse who has just lost their partner? To Christians who are living in war, in famine, in the midst of a natural disaster?

The cynic in me starts to say, "Yeah, yeah, those are words from the Scripture, but it's pretty hard to live like God will never forsake me when I am in the middle of terrifying situations." It *is* hard. But worshippers of God have hidden the truth of the word of God in their hearts. That truth is the fountain of hope, joy and love that they draw on in desert times.

When we know God's word and have committed parts of it to memory it will change our life. We will be known as those who worship in much more than in a church meeting or in private prayers. Our worship will leak out into the lives we live.

Knowing God's word is also foundational to instructing and encouraging the body. Colossians 3:16 says, "Let the word of Christ dwell in you richly as you teach and admonish one another with all wisdom, and as you sing psalms, hymns and spiritual songs with gratitude in your hearts to God."

We allow God's word to dwell in us extravagantly as we meditate on his written word, as we memorize the Scriptures, as we open our hearts to hear and listen to the Holy Spirit's voice and as we sing with overflowing gratefulness for all God has done. The word of God sustains us, encourages us and corrects us. From the overflow of God's word to us we can then teach each other; we can admonish each other with wisdom; we can sing with grateful hearts for all that we have been given.

How could we not worship him? How could we not lay down our lives pick up our cross and follow Jesus?

Ah! That's the key! The word of God *always* leads us to worship Jesus. He is the Alpha and the Omega, the beginning and the end. *He* is the Word come to life and living among us.

I love the imagery in *The Message* Bible's portrayal of John 1:1-5:

> *The Word was first, the Word present to God, God present to the Word. The Word was God, in readiness for God from day one. Everything was created through him; nothing – not one thing! – came into being without him. What came into existence was Life, and the Life was Light to live by. The Life-Light blazed out of the darkness; the darkness couldn't put it out. (Msg)*

Jesus is the *Word* of God come to life. He is the Light we follow. He is the focus of our devotion, the joy of our commitment. The Scriptures tells us that to see that Light – the *Word* of God made flesh – is to see the glory of the Son of God. "So the *Word* became human and lived here on earth among us.

He was full of unfailing love and faithfulness. And we have seen his glory, the glory of the only Son of the Father" (John 1:14 – NLT – emphasis added).

The Scriptures show us the Father, the Son and the Holy Spirit. They direct our praise, our worship, our devotion and our passion to Jesus, "the author and perfecter of our faith, who for the joy set before him endured the cross, scorning its shame and sat down at the right hand of the throne of God" (Hebrews 12:2).

The Scriptures aid us in our worship and our recognition of Jesus. But we need to be careful that we don't confuse the Scriptures with being *the Word* – or person of Jesus. Although we honour the Scriptures, we do not worship them. We worship the *One* whom they reveal – Jesus! The Scriptures point us to Jesus, but they are not the complete *Word*. The complete *Word* is only found in Jesus Christ.

Once in a time of prayer the Lord gave me a brief vision. In the vision I sat on a hillside overlooking a shallow valley. In the centre of the valley was an enormous Bible. The scene reminded me of the opening scene of the movie, *2001: A Space Odyssey* where a huge stone rises out of the valley floor attracting the apes to gather around in front of it. In my vision a huge Bible rose up out of the valley floor. It saw stood tall and mighty with many people gathered in front of its open pages. Some were reverently gazing upon it. Others knelt before it. Still others, with outstretched arms, offered praise. I felt warmed by the adoration and worship that I saw unfolding before me.

Suddenly, my perspective of the scene shifted so that I could see through the Bible to the hillside beyond. There stood Jesus with arms stretched wide open in a come-all-who-are-thirsty stance. This was awesome, I thought, until I realized that no one had gathered at his feet. No one was gazing upon his face. No one was captured by his presence. No one had even noticed him there.

The vision ended.

I was confused by this for a few minutes and cried out to God as to what it meant. For surely, if these images were from God, he had something he wanted to teach me through them. After a few moments the Holy Spirit said to me, "Gareth, sometimes even the Scriptures can become an idol when people love and serve *it* but refuse to see *me*."

At first I was repulsed by his response. But then, quickly, Scriptures came to mind which confirmed what Jesus had spoken to my heart by his Holy Spirit. Jesus says to the Pharisees in John 5:39-40, "You search the Scriptures because you believe they give you eternal life. But the Scriptures point to me! Yet you refuse to come to me so that I can give you this eternal life" (NLT).

The Pharisees were consumed by the Law of God. They studied the Scriptures, memorizing passage upon passage. They argued using the Scripture. Yet they never saw Jesus as the Son of God. They honoured, revered and served the Scriptures with their whole lives – but they missed Jesus! Even the prophets in the Old Testament understood the role of the Scriptures as secondary to Christ. Jesus answered the Pharisees with words from Isaiah. He clearly pointed out the irony of their bondage to Rome, when Jesus was in their midst – offering freedom.

He replied, 'You've been given insight into God's kingdom. You know how it works. Not everybody has this gift, this insight; it hasn't been given to them. Whenever someone has a ready heart for this, the insights and understandings flow freely. But if there is no readiness, any trace of receptivity soon disappears. That's why I tell stories: to create readiness, to nudge the people toward receptive insight. In their present state they can stare till doomsday and not see it, listen till they're blue in the face and not get it.

'I don't want Isaiah's forecast repeated all over again: Your ears are open but you don't hear a thing. Your eyes are awake but you don't see a thing. The people are blockheads! They stick their fingers in their ears so they won't have to listen; They screw their eyes shut so they won't have to look, so they won't have to deal with me face-to-face and let me heal them.

'But you have God-blessed eyes – eyes that see! And God-blessed ears – ears that hear! A lot of people, prophets and humble believers among them, would have given anything to see what you are seeing, to hear what you are hearing, but never had the chance.'
(Matthew 13:11-17 – Msg)

The disciples were different – set apart. God's Spirit gave them a soft heart and spiritual insight into the stories that Jesus told. Jesus prayed that those who loved him would retain the gift of seeing truth through the stories and in the Scriptures. He prayed that they would not become like those who only used the Scriptures as proof texts.

In my years of ministry, I have met many people in the church who were quite adept at knowing the Bible but had not yet met the living *Word* of God; people who could defend its articles and doctrines profoundly but had never been humbled by its *Author*; people who could bring all its wisdom and the judgment of the law to bear down upon the unfaithful but had never needed to receive mercy from its *Perfecter*. They could see and hear. But they didn't perceive or understand or turn to receive their healing from the *Word* of God – *Jesus*!

The Scriptures inform and instruct, encourage and convict so that we might come to see Jesus. And having seen him, we might love and worship him always. The Scriptures are our guide in that journey of worship. Knowing them intimately will help guide us to seeing and hearing him more clearly.

I certainly have not unravelled the mysteries and beauty in God's word. Nor have I fully engaged the person of the *Word* of God – Jesus – in the whole of my life. I struggle each day to walk in the little wisdom and truth I know now. But here are a few principles I've learned about knowing God's word:

1. When singing a new song ask yourself what Scripture passages the song reminds you of. Take some time later on to look them up. Then the next time you sing the song include those passages of Scripture in your reflection during worship.

   When I worship in song, I run through the Scriptures I know and draw them into the song. I see where the words of the music intersect with Bible teaching. I'll often look up phrases and try to get a deeper understanding of the song through Scripture.

2. Memorize Scripture.

   I am working at memorization. I have to say it was a lot easier on the way to church when I was seven – but I work my mind to retain the Scripture I am studying. I challenge myself with the fact that I have hundreds (maybe thousands) of songs kicking around in my brain. Surely I can learn Scripture as well.

   Sometimes I put a verse to a simple tune to help me remember it. I start with taking small passages of Scripture or single verses that have struck me. I try to go over them several times a day for several weeks. I try to pull up these Scriptures in my real life and share them with friends. As I add new verses, I go over the older ones.

   Sometimes I find it easier to memorize if I use a translation that reflects today's English. On the other hand, my roots in the King

James Version often haunt me and I tend to want to speak Scripture in 16th century English. As a side benefit, memorizing Scripture in a contemporary version helps us to more clearly reflect God's word to people in our society – most of whom didn't grow up going to church or reading the Bible.

3. Read the Scriptures.

As I read Scripture, I pause frequently to talk to God. I often have a running discussion with God, engaging in the ideas and issues that come up as I read. You see, it's more than just reading the Scriptures. It's about taking the words that I read and interacting with them, understanding them where I am today. Reading the Bible isn't a race or a challenge to accomplish ("I read through the Bible twice this year!"). I look at it as a relationship. I desperately want to get to know Jesus better. What better way than to engage in reading his word?

4. Take time to meditate on his word.

I have spent a lot of time in the past few years thinking about meditation. I try to get away from the busyness of the world in which I live and ponder the things in his written word and the things his Holy Spirit brings to light. Meditation is hard for our society. I usually drift off to sleep! But don't let drifting off to sleep occasionally dissuade you from keeping on trying. I've talked about my times with the dog and how walking helps me meditate, but there are many more opportunities during my day. Meditation is a simple quieting of the mind and the heart to think on one thing. The intense focus helps me to bring the rest of my day into perspective as well.

I often think about the men and women who have lived or are still living in countries with communist or anti-Christian governments. I've heard stories about Christians who didn't have the written word – except, perhaps, for a few chapters or verses – or those who only hear the written word of God over radio. They memorized as much as they could and then pooled their knowledge together and encouraged each other with the Scripture texts they had memorized. I wonder where would our generation be in the same situation? Would we be able to maintain an understanding of all that God has spoken? Or would we quickly become assimilated into the world's culture? Are we there already?

Know his word and know the *Word!*

"Your word is a lamp to my feet and a light for my path." (Psalm 119:105)

When you pray, you should pray like this:
'Our Father in heaven, may your name always be kept holy.
May your kingdom come and what you want be done,
here on earth as it is in heaven.
Give us the food we need for each day.
Forgive us for our sins, just as we have forgiven those who sinned against us.
And do not cause us to be tempted,
but save us from the Evil One.
For yours is the kingdom and the power and the glory forever. Amen.'
Matthew 6:9-13 (NCV)

CHAPTER THIRTEEN

PRAYER

An integral part of worship

Jesus was teaching the disciples basic life principles. When he taught on prayer, he gave them a lot of good advice. The Lord's Prayer is a simple and basic model of prayer that covers all the bases.

Jesus was direct with the disciples. He pointed out the Pharisee who stood up in temple courts and prayed with great passion so that everyone would hear him boasting to God about how good he was. Jesus was pretty clear that people like that have already received everything they would receive – attention – and nothing more (Luke 18:9-14)! He told them to pray in private, in the quietness of their own space. He went on to say that they should pray in simple words, words they used everyday. He encouraged them to ask for the things they needed everyday.

When the disciples came to Jesus and asked him to teach them to pray, he prayed a simple and direct prayer. The Lord's Prayer – or perhaps better said, the disciples' prayer – begins by acknowledging God as God. It begins intimately, calling God "Father." It starts by recognizing that God has a purpose and a plan for the world. How many times I start with my own agenda! Jesus' example of prayer starts with a clear and simple phrase of worship honouring the name of God. The last part of the prayer is personal. He prays for daily needs, forgiveness and protection.

I understand that prayer is talking to God in the most intimate way. I know that God longs for me to speak with him and to listen. I want to have a powerful and dynamic life of prayer.

But prayer is work. It takes effort to pray. I must put in physical, emotional and spiritual energy. And it takes time. Prayer is not a wimpy activity – a way out. It's work. While prayer is, at its very core, a simple conversation with God, think about the conversations that you have with someone you love. In order to have a meaningful conversation, you must be engaged with the person you are talking to.

Sometimes I talk to God like I used to talk to my children when they were four and five years old. Without listening or thinking about what I was saying, I simply talked. True conversation with God, however, is not a meaningless, mindless activity. Prayer requires that we are engaged in a relationship.

Prayer also involves discipline; silence, solitude, listening, obedience, intentionally removing ourselves from the distractions of life so that we might communicate to and with our God.

Prayer may be the most difficult work we do throughout our lives. But if we are to grow spiritually, we will pray. As we grow in prayer we begin to wrestle with who we really are before a holy God – not who we carefully allow others to see. We face our addictions and distractions head on and confess our disappointments and failures. In prayer, we begin to pull back the layers of arrogance and prideful protection. We humbly kneel before our Creator and ask for help. And he teaches us to listen for his voice.

Prayer strips us of all our excuses, our safeguards, our lies. It exposes all of our prideful notions about who we are and we stand naked and vulnerable before God. Prayer is the place where our transformational journey can begin.

In many ways this should be chapter one, because prayer is the beginning of a worshipper's journey. Prayer is how we talk to God and get to know him better. Prayer is integral to the worship process. Prayer opens up the door to God and leads us to worship. Jesus taught the disciples that the beginning and ending of prayer is honouring and worshipping God.

Pastor and author, Sammy Tippit, says:

> *The entire aim of prayer, according to Jesus, was the recognition that all of the kingdom, and all of the power, and all of the glory belonged only to God; the true goal of prayer is worship* (Sammy Tippit. "Prayer and Worship." Online posting. Sammy Tippit Ministries: God's Love in Action. 16 Oct. 2004. <http://www.gospelcom.net/glia/2001/wow/st_043001.shtml>).

Worship helps to open up windows of understanding to the God who created and sustains us. Worship draws us into the presence of God where we can hear his voice, respond to the things he is telling us and ask him for the things we need.

In July 2002, I had the privilege of speaking at Danilo Montero's *Retiro International De Adoración 2002 'De Gloria En Gloria'* (*International Worship Retreat 2002 'From Glory to Glory'*) in San Jose, Costa Rica. Many of the speakers highlighted the glory of God in their messages. That conference stunned me. I'd been teaching on worship for about eight years at the time of the conference. I *know* worship is giving God the glory. But I was blindsided by my one-dimensional thinking.

As a follower of Jesus, I have to live in a three dimensional world – I am on earth, but the spiritual world of demons and angels are very real parts of my current existence. Of course, I rarely acknowledge life beyond my own little world. I get caught in the web of my own making. Immediate problems of finances, personal relationships, opportunities for ministry and day-to-day stuff invade my mind. I pray for the things I need and want. I submit to God those requests that I have committed to praying for others. I pray for the needs of my ministry. I pray for the needs of my church and my community. But rarely, oh so rarely, do I look past my own little world and envision the glory that God desires to be shown in this world.

What does it mean to pray for God's kingdom to come? How radical is it to expect God's will to be done right here where I live – just like it's done in heaven where he is truly the King?

As a child of God, I actively live in two worlds. Prayer helps me to acknowledge that. Jesus calls us to pray that what is happening in heaven will also happen on earth. He asks us to pray that his kingdom and his desires will be known on earth just like they are in heaven. He wants his glory to be shown through our lives as we do the things we need to do.

How quickly my prayer life dissolves into a vending machine mentality, asking for things I want. Yet God asks us to centre our prayers on our desire to see the work of God accomplished in the communities in which we live.

> *Now, Lord, consider their threats and enable your servants to speak your word with great boldness. Stretch out your hand to heal and perform miraculous signs and wonders through the name of your holy servant Jesus. (Acts 4:29-30)*

This passage early in Acts is set at a time when the world had turned their back on Jesus. Few men and women accepted the teachings of Jesus; fewer still grew intimate with him. His life on earth culminated in a horrific death on a cross between two thieves. The disciples walked away in the most intense hour of their Lord and Saviour's life. They literally turned their back on Jesus, denying that they had known him. Jesus died and the world went back to what it had been before he came. It seemed as if nothing had changed.

But the drama of the death of Christ was nothing compared to the impossible joy of Christ's rising. It just was less public. Now the disciples had seen their Lord and God ascend to the heavens. He left them with the power of his Spirit and a vision to multiply God's work on earth.

When they began to tell the Good News, *"Christ has risen,"* they were threatened and persecuted and hated. The glory of God which they had experienced was smashed by the unbelief that was all around them. They prayed, not for themselves, but that God would give them great boldness to counter the lies that the people around them were saying. They wanted to speak with power and authority so that Jesus would be celebrated and praised. They were jealous for the reputation of their God, desirous for his glory.

Being jealous for the reputation of God – not only for us in the church, but for the world to see – is another hallmark of the worshipper. The worshipper is intent for the glory and the reputation of God to be known in *all* the earth.

For 13 years I participated in inner-city plunges during a week of orientation for Youth Mission International's summer missions groups. YMI is a discipleship program for Christian teens and young adults (a part of Mennonite Brethren Missions and Services International, Abbotsford, British Columbia, Canada < http://www.youthmission.org>). To be honest, most of the young men and women who came on YMI had little idea of what the seedy side of the world looked like. They had grown up in safe communities, healthy homes and protected environments. Being a Christian was just not that stunning for them because they didn't really live any differently than anyone else in their small circle.

To broaden their horizons a bit, we took them to the inner most part of Toronto. This part of the city is a spiritual wasteland, drawing a bizarre collection of very needy people. Homelessness, mental illness, sexual deviance, substance abuse and much more is right there on the streets.

We let the young adults loose on the streets in groups of three or four. Their assignment was to interact with the people, pray for the city and the people who lived there and simply soak in the atmosphere of poverty and need that was so apparent. They were not to share their faith with others, but rather to listen to the stories of people who lived on the street or in the downtown core.

After spending about six hours wandering around the downtown core that evening, we would gather in Allan Gardens Park around 11:30 p.m. Allan Gardens was well known as the meeting place for gay couples, drug dealers and gangs. We would meet together to do a short debrief of the evening. We talked about what we saw and felt. We told stories about the experiences and conversations we had. Then we would begin to intercede for the city. In our time of intercession – right there in the middle of this gay park – we lifted our prayers, our songs and our stories to worship God. We prayed that the people in the city of Toronto would recognize God for who he is. The park was dark and scary. Lights were obscured by trees. Muted corners provided ample cover of darkness for covert sexual trysts, drug deals and other illicit actions.

I will never forget the first time I participated with YMI on one of these inner-city plunges. It was in the summer of 1990. At around midnight we gathered in the middle of the park and began to worship. One of the participants broke into the middle of our worship in panic. There was a knife fight happening at the other end of the park and someone was going to get killed if we didn't do something. Randy Friesen, director of YMI at the time, suggested that we pause and ask God how he wanted us to respond before we just reacted to the need and ran into it. No sooner had we bowed our heads and begun asking when a girl spoke up. "We've been singing praise to God here. Why don't we go and worship him over there?"

We were naive and many of us had grown up in areas where wheat fields were much more familiar than concrete. But we were anxious to please God and obey his word. So 75 young men and women, most of whom had never even been in Toronto until that night, marched across the park to the fight, the whole time singing praise to God.

The guy was right. There was a knife fight and it looked like it was getting really bad. The fighters didn't even raise their heads when we came. Without any instruction or suggestion the whole group joined hands and formed a circle around the two fighters.

We kept singing.

As soon as our hands joined together, completing the circle, the two stopped fighting and fled in opposite directions. We closed in our circle continuing to worship God, sharing some of our experiences and insights and praying that the glory of God would be revealed in that city, in that park.

While we were worshipping and praying, people came from throughout the park and sat around our circle and just watched and listened. About an hour later when we finished our prayer time – close to 1:00 a.m – the group split up into twos and threes and went around talking with the people who had gathered. One group of three prairie farm boys sat down and talked with one of the knife fighters who had snuck back to see what was going on. They found out that the fight had been about drugs and money he claimed had been stolen from him.

At one point during the conversation he interrupted and asked, "Where did you guys come from?" One of the participants began to explain that he and the rest of the group were from a variety of places through Canada and were here on a missions trip. "No," he responded, "I mean tonight. I was fighting for my life – which was about to be ended – when all of a sudden there was this bright light and a pile of people standing around us! It scared the h_ _ _ out of me and I ran!"

No one from the group saw any bright light flashing. I couldn't understand how these two people fighting couldn't have heard 75 people singing at the top of their lungs – that's how terrified most of us were! But I do know that when God reveals his glory – things happen!

Recently, when I last visited Allan Gardens at night I was struck by how much it had changed since my first visit. No longer was it a dark and dingy park with low hanging shrubbery and dark corners to scuttle into. There was plenty of light. The park was clean and the shrubbery was trimmed and open. I suddenly realized that in a small way I had been a part of that change. My prayers, with hundreds of young people, over the years had brought God's attention to this park. God had begun to bring the brilliance of his light.

Has the city had a huge dramatic revival?

No. In fact, the city continues to struggle against crime, abuses and gang warfare. But in 2003, in the city of Toronto and around the nation of Canada crime rates were reported to have been falling significantly over the past ten years. Are they still higher than they were 40 years ago? Yes. But something has been happening to halt that escalation. I am not about to say that it was our prayers alone that did it. But I do believe that as more and more of God's people begin to participate in the work of prayer, jealously longing for the glory of God to be revealed in us, in our city, in our country and in our world, God is beginning to do that.

I believe that our praise and our prayer can change things. I believe that, if as a society of worshippers, we would put our hearts and our prayers to work, we could dynamically impact our communities.

How I wish that just a few of my middle-aged colleagues and friends would have had the opportunity to see the great thing that God accomplished that night. I can't imagine how most of the successful business men I know would have responded to the violence we witnessed that night. I know that most of them never see the city at night. Most of them live in a world where prayer is hardly necessary.

When we pray we are making an amazing statement. We are saying that we believe that God can and will accomplish the things he said he would do. Go back to the Acts 4:29-30 passage – God will perform miraculous signs and wonders in the name of Jesus. When we pray, we act in faith that God will do his will in our lives, our community, our world.

But prayer is work. Our prayers are actions of faith. They are statements of worship – boasting in and about the God who can and will answer – declaring to the nations and to the heavens that he is more than able and he will do it! Our prayers help to bring the glory of God into our setting. As we pray we worship and the glory of God is made visible to us, in us and through us, to others.

In many ways I am just learning to worship God in the wonder of his glory. I hardly even know what those words mean! But I am on a journey to learn how to pray. I am learning that my prayer is a lot greater when I dare to believe in God's ability to answer – for the sake of his glory!

Here are some of the things that I have been working on to build my faith in the glorious God I serve and to help me to become a better worshipper in my daily walk:

1. Ask God to teach you to pray. If you don't know how to pray about a situation – ask God to show you how you should pray.

   As humbling as it is, I have started to ask God to show me how to pray. When someone asks me to pray for them, I am learning to stop first and ask God how he would have me pray for this person or situation. I often think of the irony of my life – I am to pray, but I can't pray without God teaching me!

2. Use the Lord's Prayer as a guide to your prayers. Concentrating on the segments of the Lord's Prayer helps me to pray in a more disciplined and directed way.

   I purposely start with prayers of adoration, acknowledging that God is Lord. I open my mind and my spirit to the reality that the world has three dimensions and I acknowledge hell and heaven as real parts of that existence. I freely ask for the things that God supplies, becoming more and more cognizant that God provides all my needs – even the food I eat, which I often take for granted. I take time and go through the pain of openly admitting to my own sin and letting God take care of the places where others have hurt me. I work to let go of the things that I am hanging on to that are keeping me from loving God. I am learning to understand that God's protection is not simply from accidents and natural disasters, but from the spiritual world that is at war around me at all times.

3. Do a study on the names of God. Write down the names of God and meditate on their meanings. It will help you to have a broader understanding of the Holy God I call 'Father'.

The following is a good website to review these names for God:
<http://www.shema.com>.

4. Look up the word 'glory' or 'glory of God' in a concordance,
   Bible dictionary. If you don't have a concordance a good online
   concordance can be found at:
   <http://www.biblegateway.com/cgi-bin/bible>
   Use it to pull out verses that speak of God's glory.

I find that as I allow God to fill my heart with a greater understanding of who he is and the jealousy that he has for his glory to
be revealed on earth as it is in heaven, I begin to comprehend more
fully his desire to reveal his glory to and in me. And that always
calls me to change!

What is more, I consider everything a loss compared to the surpassing greatness of knowing Christ Jesus my Lord, for whose sake I have lost all things. I consider them rubbish, that I may gain Christ and be found in him, not having a righteousness of my own that comes from the law, but that which is through faith in Christ – the righteousness that comes from God and is by faith. I want to know Christ and the power of his resurrection and the fellowship of sharing in his sufferings, becoming like him in his death, and so, somehow, to attain to the resurrection from the dead.

Philippians 3:8-11

CHAPTER FOURTEEN

A PASSION FOR HIS PRESENCE

Wanting much more of Jesus

Knowing Christ and the power of his resurrection – that's what I want my worship, my life to be about – to know his presence at all times, to hear his words and his thoughts, to experience his ever-present hand on my life, work and relationships. I want to know that God is real in my life. I want to feel him.

Knowing God, actually feeling like God is in the room with us, is a rare and unsustainable moment. But when we feel it, when we KNOW God is there, it is a moment we rarely forget.

Experiencing the reality of God is as different as the number of people who have sought it!

For some the presence of Jesus is a feeling that envelopes like a thick fog yet with a tangible heaviness or substance to it. It is associated with intensity, intimacy and vulnerability in a time of focused worship.

For others, it is a destination you arrive at. "We were led into his presence." "I could hardly wait to be ushered into his presence." "As I walked into the room I felt the weight of his presence descend upon me." "I sensed his presence envelope me the moment I knelt in worship."

Some say they have arrived or experienced his presence when, in the quiet reverence of silence or meditation, they know the awe of "God in this place."

Others don't arrive without an ample amount of vibrant, celebrative worship that lifts their feet to dancing and their voice with shouts of praise to an awesome God.

Still others describe the presence of Jesus being revealed to them as they feed the poor, clothe the naked, meet the needs of their neighbours who have experienced loss or grief, rejoicing with those who rejoice and weeping with those who weep. For them the presence of Jesus is in the eyes of those to whom they minister.

Some say they know that Jesus is present because the Scriptures tell them so. To them, experiencing his presence is a simple act of faith in the doctrine of Emmanuel – God with us. They believe that God will never leave nor forsake them and that nothing can separate them from his love. So for them knowing the presence of God is more the activation of their faith than it is the activation of their senses.

God comes to each of us in his own unique and wonderful way. He often seems to respond to us in a way that matches who he has made us to be. To limit the description of God's presence in only one or two ways is to limit a limitless God.

If I am honest with myself, I recognize that God has demonstrated his presence to me in each of these ways at different times. If I were not listening with open ears, watching with open eyes, worshipping with an open heart – I would miss knowing God's presence many times.

I believe that God is constantly shouting out his presence to his people, but we sometimes have not tuned our senses to notice the variety of ways he lets us know that he *is* here. Or we have so narrowed our expectations of how God reveals his presence to us that we usually miss perceiving it.

In the winter of 2002, I spent three months in Guatemala attempting to learn Spanish. The first family I lived with were devout Catholics. Even though initially I could barely understand their words, I knew and saw that this family loved God. In many ways, I saw the presence of Jesus in their love and care for me – a foreigner in their home.

The season of Lent and Easter week – *Semana Santa* or *Holy Week* – is a huge event in Guatemala. Long and complicated processions wind their way through the city streets each Sunday of Lent and many times during Holy Week itself. People spend hours making amazing carpets on the streets of coloured sawdust and flowers for the procession to walk over. This is an act of giving, of making a way for the King of kings just like the people in Jerusalem did when they laid palm branches and coats on the road for Jesus to ride over on the donkey.

Others pay for the honour of carrying the large floats that depict the suffering of Christ. Women make a point of wearing high heels and warm clothes to intensify the suffering they experience. Some do it as penance for their sin. Some politicians carry the float as a way to demonstrate their humility to their constituency. Of course, like all our worship, it's not all pure. Some do it so the people in the community can see them. Others have to do it because it's necessary for their position in the community. Others simply do it because it's expected.

But whatever the rationale and despite whether I agreed theologically with the reasons behind the activity, I experienced the presence of Christ as I helped a Guatemalan family create a carpet of sawdust and roses and watched later on as people, some with tears in their eyes, carried a float depicting the crucified Christ over that same carpet – demolishing it in their path. I actually felt the weight of the words, "It was our weaknesses he carried; it was our sorrows that weighed him down" (Isaiah 53:4a – NLT). There was a visibility of the presence of Jesus in the acts of his people playing out his suffering in these processions.

If your Presence does not go with us, do not send us up from here. How will anyone know that you are pleased with me and with your people unless you go with us? What else will distinguish me and your people from all the other people on the face of the earth? (Exodus 33:15-17)

This passage in Exodus comes right after the fiasco with the golden calf. God had called Moses to the mountain for personal instruction. This meant that he had to leave the people while he ascended the mountain to speak with God. When he returned the people were worshipping a golden calf. In just a few short weeks they deserted God for an inanimate object.

God was furious!

Moses begged God to forgive the people. He had the people destroy the calf. God relented and did not destroy the Israelites, but he put a distance between them. He told Moses that he would save their lives and allow them to go on into the promised land, but he would not go with them. He even relented to the point that he agreed to give the Israelites a personal angel that would walk ahead of them to protect them and give them victory over their enemies, but God himself would stay behind. He told Moses that he was still angry with the people and that if he went with them, he might just change his mind again and destroy them on the way (Exodus 33:1-3).

But Moses refuses to go without God. No angel – no matter how powerful and capable of destroying Israel's enemies – was an adequate replacement for the presence of God himself. So he again bargains with God.

He tells God that there is no point in going ahead into the promised land if God is not with them, for without God there is nothing to set them apart from any other nation. They were God's people. Moses hung on to that distinction. The presence of God gives evidence of his leadership, his love and his life in and with his people. Moses passionately desired the presence of God in his life and in the lives of the people he led. He believed that the Israelites were nothing without God's presence.

As Christians, we are also the people of God. Our one and only distinction from all the other people on the face of the earth is the presence of God in us. God's presence is the mark on our lives that demonstrates to others that we belong to the King. We are not citizens of this world. We are strangers and aliens. We are not identified as Christ's children by the things we do – although we often get this confused. Going to church, speaking clean and pure language, not smoking, drinking moderately, carrying our Bible with us – whatever we grew up believing proved that we are Christians – are not valid indicators of our status with Christ. The only true mark of being a Christian is God's presence in our lives. We are a mirror that reflects the presence and character of God in everything that we do.

When we desire the presence of Christ in our life, we long for Jesus to be immediately apparent in everything we do. We do not naturally reflect God's character. Jesus tells us to love people – including those people who we naturally feel uncomfortable with. That means we love people exactly where they are. This is a huge challenge for me. It's so much easier for me to love the people who are a lot like me. I like to be with people who are comfortable with the same things I like. But that's not what God tells me. He tells me that I am to love the people whom he loves – with all the bizarre gaps they have in their lives.

Reflecting Jesus means that we will walk with people so they can leave their sin. We will be patient with those who sin again and again, always giving them the opportunity to come back to God. Again, this is one of the most difficult things for me to do. How can God consistently take us back when we continually walk away? But remember the story of the Israelites. Time and time again God performed miracles. As the Egyptians chased them towards the Red Sea, God opened up the water so the Israelites could walk through. Then he slammed the walls of water onto the Egyptians pursuing them, drowning most of their army. Just a few days later, as the people wandered in the wilderness, they complained to God because they were thirsty. Even though God had just done an amazing miracle, they didn't go to God nor did they trust that God would give them the water they needed. Rather they complained and whined, saying that God was not real even though God continued to be with them in the pillar of cloud and fire.

Reflecting Jesus means that we will stand up for the weak and the powerless. Jesus characterizes mercy and justice. The world reflects power and position. When we reflect Jesus in our daily lives, we protect those who cannot protect themselves. The Bible tells us that true religion is to visit those in prison and to care for the widows and the orphans. The world says that the strong succeed. God says the strong should always reach out to help the weak. The world says that if we hang around with the weak we will not get the best position. God says that position is meaningless if we lose our soul.

Reflecting Jesus means that we will confront sin and evil in us and our world. We will do it in a way that redeems the world, not simply judges and rejects. God is holy. He cannot bear sin. How much easier to simply close our eyes to sin and hope it goes away! The world in which we live is filled with activities that hurt God. That does not mean that we simply judge people. God points out people's sin in love. As God comes alongside of us and loves us, we begin to hate our sin and the closer we move to God's side, the more painful our own sin becomes.

A passion for the presence of Christ in our everyday lives enables us to understand his love for the world. When we begin to understand how much he loves the sinner we will begin to experience his presence as we worship, as we meditate, as we reach out and as we love our neighbours. And when we love and meet the needs of people we come in contact with everyday, we will begin to know his presence more in every act, every thought, every prayer, every song.

I love it when I feel the presence of God in a strong emotional way. Sometimes, especially after a lengthy time without that feeling, I find myself longing for it deeply. But I am coming to more fully understand that's not the only way he reveals himself or wants to reveal himself to me. He invites me to see him and perceive him in many different places, experiences and circumstances. He encourages me to see him in all that I do. He is eager for me to know him in all ways and not to limit the expression of his presence to me and in me.

If God's presence is to be the indication mark of God in my life to others, then I had better be doing more than seeking his presence in the midst of the gathered community of believers. I need to become desperate for God to reveal his presence to me in every circumstance, everyday. I need to reflect God's character at work, in the grocery store, on the hockey rink, in situations of conflict.

Here are a few things I've done to develop a passion for his presence:

1. Ask God to reveal himself to you each day.

   Sounds simple enough, right? And it is. But life has a way of simply happening. I forget to ask. I meander through the day hopefully being surprised by the presence of God rather than looking for him.

2. Ask yourself, "Where do I see God's activity, his handiwork, in the ordinary?"

I try and do this frequently throughout my week. But I have to be conscious of looking for God. I also have to know God more and more so that I am able to recognize him.

3. Try to keep track of when you haven't known his presence in your life and ask what circumstances might have blinded you from seeing him.

Some weeks are nuts. I seem to be moving from one thing to the next without stopping. I get so caught up in my daily life that I don't see God at all. I shouldn't be surprised at all – because I have missed looking out for him. When I recognize what has happened I begin to look for ways to create space for God to make his presence known to me again; silence for meditation; quiet reflection on his Scriptures; a walk in the park with an eye and ear open for what he wants to show me; becoming aware of the conversations that I have with others and how God may be wanting to communicate something of his presence within them.

4. Try to broaden your perspective of what his presence is or looks like by asking people in different life stages, from different denominations and different experiences to tell you about how they have witnessed God's presence in their daily lives. This is a little risky.

I meet many people in my travels. They have amazing stories to tell about how God has met them. But too often I meet people who close their minds and hearts to different ways of God acting in their lives. The charismatics see less charismatic people as unemotional and untouched by God. Sometimes they even believe that others have not even met God because they don't explain their relationship in the same ways or words. The less charismatic Christians are skeptical of the faith and lives of those who are charismatic, often suspicious that they have accepted untruths and are living purely on emotionalism. To some he speaks with a whisper or thought. To others, he speaks with imagery and colour. And to others he speaks through people.

Remember that God speaks to people in many, many different ways. Be open to listening to others and letting their relationship with God touch your life.

5. Pray that God would reveal his presence to you, wherever you are. God is there. He will show up in unexpected times. He loves you and he wants you to know him – to walk with him each day.

You are a chosen people, a royal priesthood, a holy nation,
a people belonging to God, that you may declare the praises of him
who called you out of darkness into his wonderful light.
Once you were not a people, but now you are the people of God;
once you had not received mercy, but now you have received mercy.
Dear friends, I urge you, as aliens and strangers in the world,
to abstain from sinful desires, which war against your soul.
Live such good lives among the pagans that,
though they accuse you of doing wrong, they may see your good deeds
and glorify God on the day he visits us.
1 Peter 2:9-12

CHAPTER FIFTEEN

WORSHIP THAT WITNESSES
God's presence sets us apart from those around us

We are made to worship. Peter tells the early church: " . . .we are living stones being built into a spiritual house as priests who offer our sacrifices of worship to God" (1 Peter 2:5). In Romans 12:1-2, Paul instructs the church to give up their bodies, all of their life, physically, emotionally and spiritually, as a living sacrifice in a spiritual act of worship. Giving our lives for worship means that we give up our citizenship on earth. Although we live in the world, we are to live as strangers and aliens, refusing to live as those who do not know Christ (1 Peter 2:10-12).

Why? So that the people who live in the world with us will see the good things that we do and they will acknowledge that our God is the God of power and faithfulness.

Limiting the act of worship to a segment of singing on a Sunday morning limits God in our lives. While the times of corporate worship in songs and hymns are critical to our growth and spiritual food, they are only a part of worship. True worship spills out from our lives everyday, in everything we do.

True worship, like true worshippers, never stays in the church. It leaks out into the community. Its fragrance is pungently sweet in our world. Think about it. In a world that is frightened of the future, we stand firm on the rock of our salvation, confident that God is in total control. In a world that is sick with destroyed relationships, substance and physical abuse, we rest in the arms of a God of pure love. In a world where sickness destroys bodies and minds, we are healed by the power of God.

A true worshipper's desire is to flavour the world with a taste so sweet and so tempting that those around them cannot help but be drawn to taste from the same well. True worship impacts our world.

True worship impacts our witness and our witness impacts the nations. Because we worship, we tell the story of a great and powerful God. Because we share our story, those around us experience change. Ultimately, the telling of that story radically impacts the nations. Sometimes, in our very small lives, we forget the stories of our God. Yet our history is filled with glimpses of worshippers who acted out of their passion and responded to needs through worship.

Ludwig von Zinzendorf was a passionate worshipper. In 1731, while attending the coronation of Christian VI in Copenhagen, the young Count met a converted slave from the West Indies, Anthony Ulrich. As Anthony spoke of the struggles of his people, Zinzendorf was overcome by overwhelming compassion and invited him to come back to his estate in Moravia and share this need with the students there.

During an evening of worship and testimony, two young men, Leonard Dober and David Nitchmann, were prompted by the Holy Spirit and went to St. Thomas to live among the slaves and preach the gospel. The men were not wealthy nor did they receive funds to go. So they sold themselves into slavery in order to be able to preach the gospel to other slaves. The one young man's passion was so great that he left the woman to whom he was engaged, to follow God's call to the mission field (Rev. John Jackman. "Count Nicholas Ludwig von Zinzendorf." Online posting. Zinzendorf: The Count Without Borders. 16 Oct. 2004. <http://www.zinzendorf.com/countz.htm>).

King David rarely hid his worship. He spoke boldly of his love for God to the Jews and to the nations around. In Psalm 57:9, David says, "I will praise you, O Lord, among the nations; I will sing of you among the peoples." For David, worship and praising God through psalms was critical. David's desire was that his life and full trust in God would draw the nations around him to worship God. Without embarrassment David worshipped in the street. His wife watched from the palace window and cringed at David's mindlessness to his kingly dignity. But before David was a king, he was a worshipper. His lifestyle of worship drew the nations to worship God as well.

We are missing a critical component of worship when we cut off the world from watching us. Worship is not for the church alone, worship is for the world to see. For when the world sees us worship in truth and love, they too will be drawn to praise the God of gods. When God's people are like 'Davids' before the living God, the world sits up and takes notice.

WOW! Imagine the simplicity. God tells us that if we live as true worshippers, without any effort we will become evangelists. By our very lives of worship we bring the Good News to those around us. That's a perspective of evangelism that many of us have forgotten in the systems and theologies of evangelism that have developed over the years.

David believed that God would draw unbelievers to himself through an authentic worship experience. "He put a new song in my mouth, a hymn of praise to our God. Many will see and fear and put their trust in the LORD" (Psalm 40:3).

You see, worship is the goal of evangelism – it's not a number game. Evangelism is the power of worshippers multiplying and exploding with God's praise – inviting others to join in the celebration!

In John 4:23, Jesus says that the Father is seeking worshippers. That's what he expects from his creation. D. Martin Lloyd Jones writes that "the supreme object of the work of evangelism is to glorify God, not save souls" (D. Martin Lloyd Jones, *The Presentation of the Gospel* [London: InterVarsity Press, 1949] pp. 6-7). All creation was created to give praise and glory to God.

Worship drives our witness. Someone has said that worship is the transmission between the power of the Holy Spirit and the wheels of action and proclamation. Although witness is one of the central tasks of the church, it is worship that 'drives' the witness not vice versa. Gerrit Gustafson says: "If God himself becomes our goal – even above evangelism, we will become better evangelists" (Gerrit Gustafson, 'Worship Evangelism.' (*Charisma and Christian Life,* Oct.1991: 49).

I had been ministering throughout central California for about eight straight days. God was there and he had pulled through in some amazing ways. But I was tired. I was looking forward to having five hours on my flight from San Jose to Toronto. I got on the plane and settled in to read a good book. I looked around. Yes! The plane was only half full, my row was empty! I could just read and relax the whole trip home. Awesome!

But just before the doors shut a gentleman rushed in. There were tons of empty seats to choose. What are the chances that he sits down beside me?

Very, very high!

'Henry' started right into a conversation. Now, normally, I love the serendipitous conversations I have on the plane. But I had just finished eight, 17-hour days of constant interaction with people. I wasn't interested in a conversation – I had a book to read! So I answered in monosyllables, hoping that he'd get the idea that I just wanted to be left alone. He didn't.

I stuck my head deeper in the book. He still didn't get it. Oblivious to my attempt to ignore him, he kept talking and asking questions.

I knew he would eventually get to the question that almost always stopped conversations, "So, what do you do?"

There are a lot of ways to answer that. On days that I want to open the doors to more conversation I say something like: "I'm a musician." (People love to think they are sitting beside someone famous.) If I want to feel professional and continue a business conversation, I say something like: "I am a consultant and work with organizations who specialize in long-term life investments." (Could be any motivational speaker, but the fact that I am on a plane carrying a laptop, a PDA and cell phone gives credence to my ability.) If I want to be interesting, I say: "I work as a motivational speaker for young people – encouraging them to make the best choices for their lives." (The grey hair throws them off at first, but hey, they think it's pretty cool that such an old guy can still relate to kids.) If I want to impress them about the size and quality of the firm I work for, I might say, "Our CEO is a great guy who literally lays his life down for his people; and we also have an awesome retirement plan." (Who wouldn't want to engage in a conversation with someone who has an 'in' for a great career move?) And that way, conversation continues.

But this trip, I decided to simply come out with the straight answer. It didn't take him long to get to the question. I said: "I'm a pastor who works with churches and Christian groups in the area of worship throughout Canada, the United States and Central and South America."

There, I thought, that will shut him up so I can get back to my book.

But it didn't deter him in the least. He just ploughed through it, taking up the conversation. "I'm not a Christian," he told me, "and actually, except for my parents having me baptized as an infant in the Roman Catholic church, I have never ever been to church. My wife and I got married at a justice of the peace. But I am a good person."

And he had the facts to prove it. Henry went on to explain that he had been married to his wife for 30 years and had never been unfaithful. They had raised a daughter who had never rebelled. They regularly gave to charitable causes. They recycled and composted!

"Now tell me," he said, determined to make this conversation work, "what is your religion all about?"

I started out with explaining that I preferred to see my beliefs as developing a relationship with Jesus – the Lover of my soul – as opposed to it being a religion.

"But your religion has a lot to do with sins and obeying rules and stuff, right?" Pretty typical. We Christians have pretty much given the impression that our belief system is enhanced by the number of things we say, "No" to.

So I explained that, like him, I had been married to my wife for many years. Because I am interested in making that relationship as good as it can get, I am quick to curb habits that are an annoyance to my wife. "I don't try to change my habits because Gayle will leave me if I don't," I said. "I change them because of my love for her. In the same way, because I want to develop a love relationship with Jesus, when I do things that displease him he lets me know that it isn't good for our relationship and I want to change because of my love for him."

"Besides," I continued, "if it were just about keeping the rules, the Pharisees were better than anybody else in the Bible at keeping them religiously. They had over 200 rules about food alone! And yet, Jesus said to them, 'You have heard that it was said, 'Do not commit adultery.' But I tell you that anyone who looks at a woman lustfully has already committed adultery with her in his heart'" (Matthew 5:27-28).

Henry's eyes opened as wide as saucers and he exclaimed, "Oh sh_t! I guess I'm not as good as I thought I was!"

For the rest of flight we talked about a life with Jesus, the connection between Christians and the Jews, how the Muslims fit into the picture and much more. At the end of the flight he told me he had never actually read anything in the Bible. Henry's wife was struggling with cancer and he found himself looking for a Bible in the hotel rooms that he stayed in – but none ever seemed to be there. I promised that I would send him a Bible.

I sent him a New Testament Bible and kept in touch for about a year via email until his email changed and I lost track of him. I don't know if he ever accepted Jesus as his Saviour, but I am convinced that God continues to pursue Henry and love him and open up his word to him as he reads – getting to know him better until one day he too, calls him "Lord."

We need to do a quick check . . . . Is God our goal? Is the essence of our lives and our lifestyles designed to be, like Paul encourages, so that we may *know* Christ better?

Joseph Carroll, in his book, *How to Worship Jesus Christ,* speaks of the *passion* of the apostle Paul, citing Philippians 3:8-10. "Christ was his goal. To win Christ, to know Christ, to love Christ, to have intimate fellowship with Christ, this was his ruling passion" (Joseph Carroll, *How to Worship Jesus Christ* [Chicago: Moody Press, 1984] pp. 24-25).

Then Carroll goes on to describe what evangelism is like without this ruling passion, this worship of Jesus Christ:

> *Have you ever noticed in the Pauline epistles that Paul never urges Christians to witness nor has he anything to say about foreign missions? Nothing! How interesting! If you have to constantly be telling people to witness, something is wrong with them. If you always have to be pumping up people to get them interested in foreign missions, something is wrong with the people. What is Paul always doing? He is consistently bringing you to Christ and leaving you with Christ. When Christ is central in the heart of the person, what does the person want to do? They want to tell others about Jesus, and they will do so effectively. Let Jesus Christ be central in the heart of a person, and they are going to be burdened and troubled because millions have never heard of Christ. It is going to disturb them and bring them into action. What they need is not more exhortation: they needs Christ.*
> (Caroll, *How to Worship Jesus Christ*, 25)

We must come to terms with this truth: although evangelism is one of the central tasks of the church, it is worship that 'drives' evangelism, not vice-versa.

In the previous chapter we looked briefly at Exodus 33:14-17. Moses responds to God's decision to abandon the people and let them go off with an angel to guide them, but God would not go. Moses says, "How will anyone know that you are pleased with me and with your people unless you go with us? What else will distinguish me and your people from all the other people on the face of the earth (except your presence)?" The presence of God in our lives sets us apart from our non-believing neighbours. This does not happen because we do it, it happens because the presence of God in us, by his Holy Spirit, makes us different. Our desire to worship God helps us choose to live holy lives. By cultivating a listening ear to his Holy Spirit's still, small voice we take time to help out a neighbour. When we begin to see Jesus in the 'least of these', we invite a homeless person out for a meal or give our second coat to someone who has none. As those who love God, we do things that are very strange to our world.

While pastoring in Cariboo Bethel Church in Williams Lake, BC, we had many opportunities of seeing visitors to the church give their lives to Jesus. One lady, 'Beth', came into the church one Sunday morning quite unintentionally. She and her two kids had been down at the playground and were heading back towards their home when they heard the songs of worship spilling out of the doors of the church.

She found herself attracted and intended only to look through the doors to see what was happening. But she found herself walking into the church, up the centre aisle and sitting down in the front pew with her two children. Through the remainder of the praise and worship singing she actually turned around and watched the congregation giving their praises to God, lifting their hands, kneeling in reverence or repentance and dancing in celebration.

Alex Campbell, the senior pastor, preached an excellent sermon and in concluding added, "If you are new here today and have been experiencing love in this place, you need to know that it's the love of Jesus. And if you would want to have that love for yourself, just come forward at the close of this service and we would love to pray with you to receive his love."

Beth came forward and accepted Jesus as her Saviour.

At her baptism later that month the pastor asked her what it was in his sermon that convinced her that she needed Jesus. She responded, "Oh, I don't remember anything you said except that at the end when you said the love in this place was the love of Jesus – it immediately made sense! That's what I had been drawn to! That's what I had seen on the faces of the people – I just didn't know what it was until you said it. And I really wanted that for myself."

Over the next few months Beth brought her friends to the church. Her invitation was simple. She didn't say, "Come to this church that has this great worship band," or "Come to this church that has a great preacher," or "Come to this church that has a great children's ministry program," – all of which could have been said about the church. But she invited them to come to a place where they could feel the love of Jesus. Many of them came. And many of them felt the love of Jesus and responded to become worshippers of him as well.

What better testimony of worship that witnesses to the presence of Jesus in us! How much more could our worship of God in our lives and our living make an impact to our neighbours, our communities, our cities and our world? When our worship of God impacts the way we live, our conversations with people, our spending habits, our jobs, the world begins to take notice.

Peter sums it up in a simple statement:

> *People who do not believe are living all around you and might say that you are doing wrong. Live such good lives that they will see the good things you do and will give glory to God on the day when Christ comes again. (1 Peter 2:12 – NCV)*

Here are a few thoughts I've had and some things I do to help my worship to witness:

1. Try and make sure that your worship is not just in song but also in thought and action throughout the whole day.

I try to look for the 'fingerprint' of God on the events of each day. It's kind of like those magic eye pictures. This may be a little retro for some of you, but you know those pictures that you had to squint or do something tricky with your eyes and the suddenly, like magic, another image appears in what seemed to be random patterns. I'm often surprised what I see when I take the time to look.

2. If you are a worship leader for Sunday morning worship times, ask the Holy Spirit to help you choose songs that declare clearly who Christ is for those who may not know him. Most people who come to check out a service of worship are looking for some kind of spiritual connection. Songs that help the congregation connect with the object of their worship will also demonstrate that connection to seekers.

3. Attempt to see every opportunity that arises as an opportunity to respond to people in a way that opens doors for the Holy Spirit to have an impact on them. You know, a lot of people are watching us who we don't even know.

My wife, Gayle, was a camp counsellor in her teens. She was young, carefree and pretty unconcerned about the rules and regulations. But she was passionate about telling the campers that they could have a relationship with Christ. Years later a young woman in her early twenties came to our home and told her that it was her passion and love for God that impacted her that summer. Who knows what our response to interruptions and disruptions will have on those who are watching us.

4. Try to be liberal with your praise and open about your relationship with Jesus, recognizing that people are more interested in relationships than in religion. Describing your life in Christ as a series of things that he doesn't approve of nor want us to do, is

like a husband telling you that he really loves his wife, but constantly complains about her. Do you love Jesus? Then act as his lover. Boast about him. Be able to tell others what you love best about your relationship with him. Encourage others with words and actions that reflect your love for Jesus.

5. Make yourself available for God to use in impacting others.

As much as I love to read while I fly, I try to make myself available for that travelling partner who just wants to talk. Who knows what seeds God will plant through us because we choose to give praise to him through our testimony of his faithfulness to us!

Your attitude should be the same that Christ Jesus had.
Though he was God, he did not demand and cling to his rights as God.
He made himself nothing;
he took the humble position of a slave and appeared in human form.
And in human form he obediently humbled himself even further
by dying a criminal's death on a cross.
Philippians 2:5-8

CHAPTER SIXTEEN

A WORSHIPPER'S HEART
Embracing brokenness and humility

For 13 years I have had the joy of serving Youth Mission International – a youth and College & Career discipleship/missions program based in Canada and the United States. Throughout those years I have met thousands of young people. Each encounter is unique.

One of the most moving spiritual moments as we prepare to serve God through short term missions is washing one another's feet. One night about 2000 years ago, Jesus wrapped a towel around his waist and knelt before each one of his disciples and washed their dusty feet. It's hard to understand what that means in our culture. While most of us in North America are showered and perfumed and powdered and keep our feet in pretty clean condition, the people in Jesus' day had dirty, dusty feet. The lowest class of servant in the household was delegated to wash the feet of the guests. That's why some of the disciples balked at their Lord and teacher humbling himself to serve them by washing their feet. But Jesus used it to demonstrate servant leadership – a model they were also to follow.

While at one time foot washing was a common practice in the church, we rarely humble ourselves in similar ways in the modern church. Even though our feet are a lot cleaner than they were back in Jesus' day, there is something uncomfortable about having another person remove your socks and shoes and wash your feet. There is something inside me that wishes I had known ahead of time so I could have pre-washed my feet and put foot powder in my smelly shoes! In fact, most people I've talked with about this practice would rather wash another person's feet than have their own feet washed.

Foot washing is a humbling act of service.

In my denomination's theology, foot washing is one of the three sacraments or ordinances that we ostensibly observe – along with communion and baptism. Yet I have never participated in a congregational foot washing service in any of the churches in which I have been a member.

Foot washing is an invasion of personal space. It's uncomfortable and humiliating not to mention hard to organize in a church setting. So, generally, we choose not to participate in it.

And yet, Jesus did this for his disciples.

But we say, "For Jesus, it had practical significance because people in his day walked around on dusty roads with only sandals on their feet. Their feet became dirty so washing them was a very practical thing to do. It's not the same for us in our day. "In our day," we say, "people take many baths or showers each week. The environment we live and work in is clean, so washing feet has no practical purpose for us today. We have paved roads and ride in clean cars and so we arrive at friends' homes without the need for cleansing our bodies of the dirt and grime like they did in Jesus' day."

"Washing each other's feet is only symbolic of a servant attitude towards our fellow believer. Today, we can serve each other in more practical ways – ways which are as relevant to our societal norms as washing feet were relevant to Jesus' societal norms. We 'wash each others' feet' today by doing other kinds of service for each other like looking after our friends' house and yard while they are on vacation, bringing food to the shut-in or the ill, putting on wedding and baby showers, or babysitting for a friend without charge."

I understand each argument. All those things are wonderful ways to care for each other out of love for Christ. And we should be doing these things for each other. I also realize that washing feet in Jesus' day was a common and necessary duty. But it wasn't a duty that everybody did. Even in Jesus' day it was a humiliating task saved only for the lowest of servants. It was something that no servant aspired to. It was seen as demeaning, degrading and repulsive even by the servants themselves (actually, *servant* sounds much more humane than *slave*, the more common usage in those days). And that's precisely the reason Peter had such a difficult time with it – a master should never wash his disciple's feet! Yet Jesus did (John 13:4-17)!

So, this reality begs the question: "What are we doing today that practically assists our fellow believers, meeting their need, while at the same time is seen by our society as demeaning, humiliating, perhaps even scornful?"

I'm still seeking an answer for that. Perhaps it really is nothing more than getting on our knees and washing our friend's feet. I think though, that there are many ways in which we are humbled when we openly express our faith in the world in which we live. Our society boasts of tolerance and political correctness. Most people see my expression of faith in ONE God and ONE Lord as delusional! Our society is very sure that there are many ways to heaven – if they even believe in a higher power at all.

You know, perhaps it isn't washing people's feet in a literal fashion. Perhaps it's being faithful to walking alongside of people even when their life is a mess. Perhaps it's refusing to say, "I knew it. I told you so."

I know so many Christian friends who struggle and struggle with issues in their lives: marriage relationships that are hell on earth, depression that's robbing their sleep and making them unable to work, secrets of past relationships that keep them from fully experiencing the joy in their current relationships. I also know that many of them refuse to share those struggles with others because they are terrified of rejection.

True worshippers embrace brokenness.

When we stretch out our arms to catch one who is falling, we are expressing the love of God. Yes, many times I can see the pattern. I know that the decisions and relationships my friends are making will destroy them. Often I try to say something, but my words are tossed aside.

But when they fall, I need to be there in their brokenness.

In a prayer service, the pastor called us to listen to God for a name and then to go to that person and encourage them. It all seemed a little vague and uncertain – frankly, it seemed a little weird. Gayle was with me and she thought it was even more weird than I did because, well, she's a lot more distrustful when things aren't in some order that makes sense to her. But God asked her to go sit with a young man and to simply cry with him.

I have rarely seen Gayle cry. She grew up in a stoic Mennonite family and maintains that tradition with tenacity. But, by the grace of God, she went to the young man, sat beside him and instantly started to weep.

That was it . . . she simply wept with him. When she got up, she felt that the work that God had wanted done, was done. During that moment of cooperative weeping, God's Spirit allowed this young man to pour out his heart and let go of a bunch of hurts that were killing his spirit.

I stood in front of my congregation at Kitchener Mennonite Brethren church one Sunday morning. While I stood there, God's Spirit pummelled me. I saw the longing of God for the congregation. I felt the painful tears that God had for a people that refused to listen to his words. I opened my Bible, set out my notes, looked into the eyes of the congregation and began to weep. I tried several times to control myself so that I could begin preaching, but finally gave up and asked someone for a tissue. For the next 15 minutes I stood in front of the congregation and wept. Then I sat down.

Worship, at times, is consumed by the humility of a broken heart. Without a painful encounter, without a broken spirit, we cannot fully understand the extraordinary love God has for us.

We are not placed into the world for position, wealth or power. We are here to give ourselves to God and each other in humility and brokenness as we serve one other. With this attitude we embark on the journey the Lord has prepared for us, embracing the heart of Jesus who "did not come to be served, but to serve, and to give his life as a ransom for many" (Mark 10:45).

In the fall of 1996, I was leading worship for a conference with Jack Deere at Cariboo Bethel Church – my former pastorate in Williams Lake, BC, Canada. I was in a prayer meeting a few days before the conference with the elders and growth group leaders and spouses. Part way into the prayer meeting I felt the Lord's prompting to go and wash a friend's feet. I opened my eyes slightly and looked over at his feet. Allan was wearing cowboy boots! Well, I thought, that certainly can't be the Lord's voice – how would I ever get those boots off?

I passed off the thought and continued to pray. But it kept coming back stronger and stronger. Finally, after struggling for about half an hour I got up and went to the kitchen to get a basin of water. I had no sooner begun running warm water into the basin when Louise, the youth pastor's wife, came into the kitchen and asked what I was doing. When I replied that I was going to wash Allan's feet she replied, "No you're not! I am supposed to!"

Surprised by her comment, I realized that God had called out another person to support me in what he had asked me to do. We came into the room during a time of silence and went up to Allan and told him that we felt God prompting us to wash his feet. "Would that be okay?" we asked. He began to cry out saying, "No! No!"

As we began to wash his feet he began to manifest some demonic stuff. What a shocker! But without going into too much detail, over that evening and the next night we were able to help Allan come face to face with some of his pain and some misconceptions about God that the enemy had been able to delude him with for years.

When we are willing to humble ourselves and act on God's prompting, miracles happen. Praise the Lord for the humility of foot washing that led to a release for a brother in the Lord! What a privilege to be used as God's servant in accomplishing what he desired that night!

All of Jesus' life was an example of his humility and servanthood. The apostle Paul reminds us of Christ's humility and brokenness in many of his letters, calling the church to die to self (Galatians 2:19-20; Philippians 3:9b-14; Romans 6:5-14); to prefer others (Philippians 2:1-5); to forgive each other (Colossians 3:12-15); to humbly serve each other (1 Peter 5:5-7; Romans 15:5-7).

When we worship Jesus with our lives, moving beyond our pride to give to others, allowing ourselves to experience his humility and brokenness in us, we catch a glimpse of a life that was fully sacrificed in every way for us. We see our self-perceived importance in light of his sacrificial giving and once again perspective is achieved. Without him we are nothing. With him, *he* is everything!

Paul encourages the Philippians, and us, to take on the attributes of Christ who:

> . . .*had equal status with God but didn't think so much of himself that he had to cling to the advantages of that status no matter what. Not at all. When the time came, he set aside the privileges of deity and took on the status of a slave, became human! Having become human, he stayed human. It was an incredibly humbling process. He didn't claim special privileges. Instead, he lived a selfless, obedient life and then died a selfless, obedient death – and the worst kind of death at that: a crucifixion. (Philippians 2:6-8 – Msg)*

Selfless service isn't always seen among leadership. Somehow with leadership comes position, power and privilege. It is rare that a Christian leader walks into a ministry with the hope of power and status. Most are genuinely called to service for God and desire with all their hearts to serve him, the church family and the community around them. But Satan messes with us. He convinces us that our call and our skill at teaching, praying and leading, deserve honour. In time, if the leader does not keep close contact with God and in good fellowship with other men and women of faith, their sense of the holy and pure is dulled by the glitter of earthly praise.

We see it all the time.

Thankfully, that's not always the case. I have a friend named Steve Lightle – a messianic Jew who has been mightily used of God throughout North America, Europe and Asia helping to prepare the way for Russian Jews (and others) to return home to Israel. I will never forget the day when a small group of leaders and participants were sitting and talking around a table following lunch. After a while someone asked, "Hey, where did Steve go?" We found him in the kitchen doing dishes and chatting with the cooks!

I was strongly impacted by Steve's example of humble service. Here was a man who has seen angels and demons, who has seen God raise the dead to life again, who has lived a life in the Spirit that most can only dream of – a man who has spoken in some of the largest churches in the world and has stood before governments in a variety of countries delivering a strong message from the Lord – in the kitchen washing dishes!

I have tried to model that humble servanthood in my leadership as I travel around, looking for ways to help others out no matter how menial the task might seem. You know what I've found? You get into some of the best conversations with people as you serve them and serve with them in the kitchen! You find that people are more open to what you are saying when you are willing to walk for a while in their shoes.

And it's enjoyable!

Jesus told the disciples:

> *If I, your Lord and Teacher, have washed your feet, you also should wash each other's feet. I did this as an example so that you should do as I have done for you. I tell you the truth, a servant is not greater than his master. A messenger is not greater than the one who sent him. If you know these things, you will be happy if you do them. (John 13:14-17)*

I pray that you would experience the gift of humility, seeing God in your fellow believer who serves you. Get in touch with Jesus' humility and brokenness.

1. One way to experience servanthood in a new and fresh way is to wash each other's feet. It is the beginning of learning to humbly submit to serving each other at deeper levels. Perhaps in a small Bible study group or during a time when you are camping or on retreat, make time to look at the John 13 passage and participate in washing each other's feet and praying for each other.

   A friend of mine proposed to his girlfriend by washing her feet, committing himself to serve her in their marriage. What a wonderful way to demonstrate the humility and love of Christ who gave himself up for his bride – the Church.

2. As a leader, always look for where you can help out in your free time.

   I try to ask myself. "How can I make someone else's day go a bit better because I helped carry a load with them for a time?" I think that people are more willing to follow a person who doesn't see themselves as above them or above stooping to help with lowly tasks. True freedom is the freedom to be all things in Christ. I can speak in front of a crowd of people, but I can also wash the dishes in a small kitchen.

3. Periodically, ask God to examine your heart to see if there is pride or a lust for power and position that is blinding you from being a humble servant leader.

   I find that it's a good practice to participate in because it allows the Holy Spirit to humble me and to instruct me in better ways of leading. I have also found that God, when we ask him, provides ample situations to keep us humble.

One of the Pharisees invited Jesus to have dinner with him, so he went to the
Pharisee's house and reclined at the table. When a woman who had lived a
sinful life in that town learned that Jesus was eating at the Pharisee's house,
she brought an alabaster jar of perfume, and as she stood behind him at his feet
weeping, she began to wet his feet with her tears. Then she wiped them with her
hair, kissed them and poured perfume on them. When the Pharisee who had
invited him saw this, he said to himself, "If this man were a prophet, he would
know who is touching him and what kind of woman she is—that she is a sinner."
Luke 7:36-39

CHAPTER SEVENTEEN

EXTRAVAGANT WORSHIP

From a heart of gratitude

While this woman was dripping expensive perfume over Jesus' feet, the
disciples were standing on the outskirts of the circle thinking, Man, if
this woman had donated that perfume, we could have used it to pay for
some of the expenses we have incurred since hooking up with Jesus
(Matthew 26:8-9).

Her act was an act of extravagant worship.

Since 1987, I have attempted to discover as much as possible about living
a life of worship. I have looked for ways of stretching that worship
experience I had on a Sunday morning into my daily life. I want to live, not
just as a worshipper of him, but as an extravagant worshipper.

I have attended conferences, seminars and workshops that have given me the opportunity to experiment and to experience different ways of expressing my worship. I have searched for and found powerful, anointed songs by gifted musicians that have drawn me towards my goal of extending extravagant worship to Jesus – corporately and privately. I have discovered principles of daily living that have opened my heart to worship him within the simplicity of everyday occurrences. I have read valuable books and resources that have helped to broaden my perspectives on who God is and who I am before him.

And yet, extravagant worship isn't found in any of these things.

Gathering knowledge and experience is very much a part of our humanness. We look for insight from experts. We search out the best resources. But there is no program or event that will guarantee an extravagant, responsive heart. There is no specially anointed song or gifted musician that can draw our hearts to change direction and devotion on an ongoing basis. There is no training program or conference that will arrest our lives and cause us to live as an extravagant offering to Jesus.

Should we stop going to them? Not at all. But as we search for God and look for ways of knowing him better, we have to come face-to-face with the reality that while all these things can be helpful in drawing out a hunger from deep within us, there is no magic seminar or experience that will change our hearts.

Extravagant worship comes from something much simpler – yet much more complex.

The woman who came to Jesus – while he was eating at Simon, the Pharisee's house – did not come as an invited guest. Frankly, I'm pretty sure Simon was appalled at her presence. The Pharisee had a certain stature in the community – not to be defiled by the wrong kind of company.

When the woman came to the house, she risked everything. She wasn't invited. She didn't even know if Jesus would welcome her or turn her away. She came with a gift that was precious to her. A gift that she felt was worthy of Jesus.

We don't know exactly who she was or why she sought out Jesus. We do know that the people at the dinner recognized her as sinful. As a woman, she had little right to interrupt dinner between men. As a sinful woman, she had no place being in Simon's home at all. We do know that she recognized her own sins *and* Jesus' capacity to forgive them.

The context of the passage implies that the people with Jesus were unsure if he knew she was sinful. Had he known she was sinful, they assumed that Jesus have would have pushed her away. She stood behind Jesus, tears flowing freely. She understood her own sinfulness. As Jesus reclined at the table, she poured perfume over his feet and wiped them with her own hair.

Extravagant worship does not come from experience or practice or ritual. Extravagant worship comes from a heart of gratitude. Like this woman, the worshipper who worships with extravagance has come face-to-face with the gift Jesus has given.

Grace! Only when we have received grace undeservedly, do we understand that God's incredible love gives us life when we deserved death. Only when we come to the end of all our own resources and we face our own ineptitude, are we willing to call to God to lift us out of our sin. Only when we have lost our confidence in this world, in ourselves, can we see Jesus in his fullness and let him develop our potential. Only when we understand that there is nothing that we have that is worthy of God's love and grace, can we understand his unconditional acceptance.

Simon didn't get it. Entertaining Jesus was about prestige and duty, perhaps curiosity. He offered Jesus the essence of hospitality without the humility of it. Simon saw himself as Jesus' peer, as righteous and holy as Jesus was. In many ways, Simon missed what was right in front of him. He saw Jesus as a man, not as the Saviour.

Simon had religion. He understood laws and systems. All his life he had been taught that holiness was reflected in the company he kept. So he kept good company. He was aghast that Jesus would let this woman touch him. Jewish laws were very, very clear about the holy and the impure keeping their distance.

But Jesus, as Jesus is so apt to do, turned it around on him. Jesus knew that Simon was confused. He understood that Simon did not see himself as sinful – after all, he was a Pharisee, a leader and a man of God. The woman knew she was sinful. Simon had no clue. Jesus said to Simon, ". . . her many sins have been forgiven – for she loved much. But he who has been forgiven little loves little" (Luke 7:47).

She gave an extravagant gift of thanks to Jesus because she had no other way of expressing how much she loved him.

Part of the problem of giving Jesus an extravagant offering of worship is that we tend to forget how much we have been forgiven. This woman's sins were obvious to the whole community. She was a lavish sinner!

I grew up in a Christian home. Comparatively, I'm a pretty good guy. I have never lit a cigarette or even tasted a beer! Sometimes, I get the idea that I am just the kind of guy that Jesus would have sought out – because I'm a pretty good friend.

How far from the truth.

Standing beside the purity of Jesus, the petty religious do's and don't's that I have established are pitiful. Sometimes, I am so pathetic, that I start to believe in my own righteousness – that Jesus didn't really have to die for me!

And so, often the love I extend to Jesus is little more than the love I give to a friend. But Jesus *is* God. Jesus *is* Lord. Jesus HAD to die so I could live. It's critical for me to understand how much I needed him and still need him. All those things that I have chalked up as good things in my life are nothing but filthy rags in comparison to the purity and holiness of Jesus (Isaiah 64:6). I cannot stand before God without the cloak of grace and forgiveness that Jesus daily offers me. I desperately *need* a Saviour!

While Jesus is my intimate friend, he is not like me. He is awesome in his power and holiness. My friendship with Jesus is a gift, a gift of love from a Saviour and Creator. Yes, Jesus is a friend, but he is also the Lord of the Universe. Extravagant worship comes when I get a glimpse of the depths of a Love that would compel the Creator God to leave heaven and live as a human, so he could die . . . for me. Extravagant worship begins when I realize that Jesus loves me so much that he longs for relationship with me! Extravagant worship comes when I know that Jesus' love carried my sin and covered it with the sacrifice of his own sinless blood. And he didn't have to – he did it because he loved those he created and could no longer stand the pain of watching his chosen walk in sin and darkness.

How could I withhold my love from such an extravagant Giver? How could I do anything but worship? How could I be anywhere but in the place of devotion to my Lord? Can I do less than lay my life down in service to him who laid down his life for me?

In 1993, forty team leaders and resource people sat around a circle at a Youth Mission International orientation worship service. Randy Friesen, then the director of YMI, had told me that he wanted to speak that night about developing intimacy with Jesus in our daily walk. I had selected songs I felt would invite us to a place of desiring intimacy with Jesus. The final song before Randy was to speak was a song by David Ruis called *True Love* – a song taken from the first chapter of the Song of Solomon.

TRUE LOVE

Jesus I need to know true love, Deeper than the love found on earth
Take me into the King's chambers, Cause my love to mature

Let me know the kisses of Your mouth
Let me feel Your embrace
Let me smell the fragrance of Your touch
Let me see Your lovely face
Take me away with You, Even so, Lord, come
I love You, Lord. I love You more than life
I love You, Lord. I love You more than life

My heart – my flesh yearn for You, Lord. To love You is all I can do
You have become my sole passion, Cause my love to be true

c/r 1992 Shade Tree Publishing (David Ruis)

As we finished the song and I just played softly through it once again, Joe – one of the leaders – fell to the floor on his knees and cried out, "Somebody help me!" No one moved. Again he cried out, "Somebody please help me! I can't sing this song. The words are too intimate. I can't say them – something's wrong with me! Someone please pray for me!"

A few of the other leaders and resource people gathered around and began to pray for Joe as he wept bitterly on the floor. One by one, other people in the room began to fall to their knees and call out to Jesus and wet the floor in his presence with their tears. Those who weren't facedown on the floor or praying for others sang songs of worship and praise with an intensity and abandon that could not have been manufactured.

Randy never spoke that night – Jesus did! And we responded. Two and a half hours later we finished off with a glorious song of praise to God who had reminded us of the intimacy he desires to have with us and the extravagance of his love for us. How could we have given him anything less?

Extravagant worship can only happen when we truly understand the depths of our need of God.

When Jesus came to visit Mary and Martha in their home (Luke 10:38-42), Mary left her duties as the woman of the house and simply sat at Jesus' feet and absorbed his words. Martha was livid. She had a guest and she did what was expected of her – she served him. Mary shirked her responsibility. I often wondered why Mary did what was so culturally irresponsible – sitting at Jesus' feet when her 'place' – culturally – was the place of service. Why was she so absorbed with Jesus that she had to be in his presence listening to his words – even though society and her sister frowned upon that act?

I found an interesting reference in John 11:2: "This Mary, whose brother Lazarus now lay sick, was the same one who poured perfume on the Lord and wiped his feet with her hair." And I wondered. Could Mary have been the woman who came, uninvited, to Simon, the Pharisee's house that day? Could she have been the woman who was known in the community as "a sinner?" Perhaps she was the one Jesus had declared to be forgiven!

I haven't been able to find many theologians who agree with that scenario – few even try to make that connection. But John Lightfoot (1602–1675) writes in his book, *A Commentary on the New Testament: from the Talmud and Hebraic;*

> That in view of the verb tense which is used for 'anointed' in John 11:1-2 and the fact that the town of Bethany is known as "the town of Mary and her sister Martha" not as the town of Lazarus (John 11:1) gives strong indication of a prior relationship with Jesus. It gives credence to the fact that the 'anointing' of Jesus' feet took place at sometime

in the past rather than saying it proleptically – in reference to what he was about to say in John 12:3 (John Lightfoot. 'Exercitations upon the Evangelist St. John.' Online posting. *A Commentary on the New Testament from the Talmud and Hebraic.* 16 Oct. 2004. <http://www.ccel.org/pipeline/1-html/5-lightfoot-nt_talmud/john11.htm>).

Suppose that indeed was the case – that Mary, who had been known in the town as a sinful woman, was suddenly forgiven of all her sin and restored to wholeness there at the feet of Jesus. Then no wonder she had to be at Jesus' feet! No wonder she abandoned her cultural protocol! She had been forgiven SO much! How could she be anywhere but at her Master's feet? She had been forgiven extravagantly – and her worship in return was given extravagantly!

I have been in many settings leading worship in an attempt to elicit joy and celebration for what God has done for us. Some people enter in fully. Most sing along politely. Over the years I have been in situations where, in response to a call to repentance, people have come forward to confess their sins, to lay down their burdens, to openly proclaim their need of Jesus.

Often, after that time of confession and restoration we have ended with a time of celebration. I am always amazed at the freedom with which these people express their worship and praise to God! They shout with joy, they dance with abandon, they openly weep in true gladness. You never have to encourage them to "give the Lord the praise he deserves!" They freely give it because they understand how freely God has given to them and forgiven them. Their worship is anything but meagre – it is extravagant!

The depth of our extravagance in worship is often a reflection of the realization of the gift we have been freely given in Christ Jesus. Where we understand how much that God has forgiven us, we worship him with overflowing extravagance.

Here are a few thoughts I've had and some things I do to help me worship extravagantly:

1. Don't fill your life with activities that are only outward demonstrations of a life of worship. Public worship and worship connected only to music can grow to become a 'groupie' thing. We go from CD to CD, concert to concert, conference to conference, to recreate an experience that we hope will ignite our sense of worship. Raised hands, kneeling bodies, even prostrating ourselves do not necessarily make us worshippers. Hearts filled with gratitude, giving praise from their very depth – that's worship. Extravagant worship isn't about methods or events or products or postures – it is about a love relationship with the Lover of your soul.

   You know, sometimes I see marriages that are dead or dying. I see a man and a woman living in the same house, going to dinner, entertaining friends and raising children. Yet there is little joy in that relationship. There is little laughter, little love. There is no relationship, no celebration. Going through the motions, does not make a worshipper.

2. Ask God to remind you of how much he has forgiven you.

   Sometimes I need to be reminded of how much I have been forgiven – especially when I get to feeling super-spiritual or am being blessed significantly in my ministry among others. If I forget where I have come from I may lose my understanding of how I have come to be where I am – only by the grace, love, mercy, forgiveness and unmerited favour of God through Christ Jesus.

3. Ask God to remind you of his love often as you go through your day.

As I work and play I want to always be aware of how much I am loved by Jesus. Because I travel a lot, I am away from home about 150–175 days a year. I miss my wife and family. But because I know of their love for me, I am all the more eager to never do anything which would harm or disappoint them. I want that same desire to be all the more poignant in my walk with Jesus – that even though I don't see him with my physical eyes, still I desire to live my life as an offering to him.

4. Meditate on his written word and on his character. Invite him to create in you those same characteristics.

I ask Jesus to continue to perfect his image in me – to make us one just as he and the Father are one – just like Jesus prayed:

Father, just as you are in me and I am in you. May they also be in us so that the world may believe that you have sent me. I have given them the glory that you gave me, that they may be one as we are one: I in them and you in me. May they be brought to complete unity to let the world know that you sent me and have loved them even as you have loved me. (John 17:21-23)

Our extravagant worship begins by better knowing and understanding our extravagant Saviour and Lover of our souls – Jesus.

Let love be your highest goal,
but also desire the special abilities the Spirit gives,
especially the gift of prophecy.
For if your gift is the ability to speak in tongues, you will be talking to God
but not to people, since they won't be able to understand you.
You will be speaking by the power of the Spirit but it will all be mysterious.
But one who prophesies is helping others grow in the Lord,
encouraging and comforting them.
1 Corinthians 14:1-3 (NLT)

CHAPTER EIGHTEEN

PROPHETIC ENCOURAGEMENT

Us to him, him to us, us to others

I can't even start a discussion of worship and the gifts God gives us, without setting a very clear focus. God has given you gifts through his Spirit – these are not natural talents or inclinations – they are gifts that are from the Holy Spirit, given to you because the church needs them.

But these gifts, when not founded in love, wreak havoc on the church.

So focus on this one segment for a moment: "Let love be your highest goal" (1 Corinthians 14:1 – NLT). Using your gifts without love is to severely limit their effectiveness. Without love, giftedness becomes a competition, a comparison and a conflict. We forget that our gift is given to grow the church, not to tear it apart. We foolishly become proud of a gift we have been given – as if it was something we deserved or worked to get in the first place. We did nothing to earn it. It's a gift. Yet we rate the gifts and set of a hierarchy of more important gifts. But we only have them because God is a gracious gift-giver.

It's pretty simple. While vastly over quoted and underused, 1 Corinthians 13 clearly puts the language of love in day-to-day terms:

> *Love is patient and kind. Love is not jealous or boastful or proud or rude. Love does not demand its own way. Love is not irritable, and it keeps no record of when it has been wronged. It is never glad about injustice but rejoices whenever the truth wins out. Love never gives up, never loses faith, is always hopeful, and endures through every circumstance. Love will last forever. (1 Corinthians 13:4-8a – NLT)*

Even if I take just one of the "love is . . ." phrases, I can think of way too many times that I fall far short of even coming close to acting like that. But people will know that you are a worshipper of Jesus because they see that you love one another with a love that is dynamically different than the love they see in the world.

I love the way Paul puts it. If I have the gift of speaking with great eloquence, but speak without love, I am simply an irritating and loud noise. If I can do miracles – big miracles, like throwing mountains into the sea, – but do them without love, I am nothing. If I am super philanthropic or heroically give my life as a martyr but do it without love – I have wasted the effort (1 Corinthians 13:1-3).

Love is the very essence of life as a worshipper. Without love all spiritual gifts can be falsely defined as evidence of achievement, expertise, maturity, or spiritual authority. Without love, the gifts God gives can tear apart rather than strengthen the church. Paul understood this principle well. As a Pharisee, he was trained and disciplined to carry out the law. He did it well. Never once, until he met Jesus face-to-face in that stunning moment on the Damascus road, did he even think of the people that he disciplined. He used his authority without love or mercy – only to carry out the law. He did it, ultimately, out of his own pride in his position and his own ability to maintain the law perfectly.

In 1 Corinthians 12-14, Paul lays out a framework of understanding what spiritual gifts are all about. Too often, when we study Paul's letters to the Corinthians, we pull what has come to be known as the love chapter completely out of context. Although the chapter has excellent advice and guidelines for marriage and interpersonal relationships, the core of the teaching belongs in the church and in the use of our gifts.

In chapter 14, Paul highlights the gifts of prophecy and tongues. He prays that all Christians would practice these two gifts. Then he stresses the importance of the gift of prophecy – not because he believes that tongues are less desirable, but because tongues only edify, encourage and build up the individual (unless interpreted for the body). He privileges prophecy because it edifies, encourages and builds up the *whole* body.

When we read Paul, we have to understand that his whole focus was the growth of the church. So it is paramount for him to focus on the gifts that help the church grow. The gift of prophecy is given to help others to grow in the Lord. The gift of prophecy encourages and comforts them (1 Corinthians 14:3). Prophecy then, is to be desired along with all those gifts that help to build up the church (1 Corinthians 14:12).

Previously, in chapter eight, I talked about the still, small voice of the Holy Spirit who prompts us to action. Everyone who has given their lives to Jesus and received his indwelling Spirit upon conversion has heard the voice of the Spirit from time to time. While his voice may not always be experienced in the same way all the time or in the same way with every believer, most of us have at one time or another obeyed his prompting. As we obey a prompting from God and carry out the action, another person receives encouragement because we are willing to obey.

For example, many people I have spoken with have told me of times when they have been awakened in the middle of the night with someone's name coming to mind and a sense that they needed to pray for them. Later they have found out that the person they prayed for was indeed in need of prayer at that time. God used their obedience to pray in an hour of need to build up, strengthen, encourage and help these people during an important or difficult time in their lives.

Others have told to me that they have received a personal visit, phone call, letter, or email from a Christian friend who just 'felt' the need to encourage them at that particular time. The result was that each one was encouraged – the giver and the receiver! Each was built up! Each was strengthened in their spiritual walk with the Lord!

Still others have occasionally, while reading Scripture, had a verse 'jump out' at them, and immediately, they knew that they needed to share it with a friend. When they did, it was clear that this verse was an encouragement for their friend.

Sometimes the person with the prophetic prompting from God doesn't have clue as to what it means. Early in the years of being a youth pastor, Gayle struggled with a bunch of stuff. One Sunday morning, a woman she hardly knew handed her three Scripture references and told her that God had told her, "Give Gayle these verses." The woman shrugged and said, "I have no idea what they mean – but God does." Those three little verses dynamically changed Gayle's life. Each verse blatantly pointed to sin that needed cleaning up. While she was a little unsettled by the fact that God had pointed out her sin to another person, she felt an overwhelming love from God – he cared enough to come after her when she had wandered away. And he used a sister in the Lord who had enough faith to obey.

There was no judgement and no confrontation, just a simple gift of a few verses. Maybe it seemed like a little thing – but it was a miracle.

Prophetic encouragement is simply a process of listening to God and responding to others with what he asks of us. That is the essence of worship. As a part of our walk of worship we open ourselves up for God to use – as a living and holy sacrifice (Romans 12:1). We allow him to interrupt our daily routine for purposes that he might want – to use us to encourage others.

Listening is a part of the worship process; us to him, him to us, us to others. We listen for what God might want to say to us and through us to others. As we listen and learn to hear his voice we begin to become more aware of what he wants to say and do. He makes us aware of what our needs and other's needs really are. When we listen to his voice he will sometimes call us to perform an act of service or kindness for another person, to speak to and encourage a fellow believer, or to be the voice, hands and feet of Jesus in society.

I teach at a variety of Discipleship Schools in Canada and the United States. I often do an exercise in prophetic encouragement with the students. I divide the class into pairs. Then we take 5–10 minutes of silence asking God to use us to speak a word of encouragement to our partner.

Sometimes a verse of Scripture comes to mind and an application of how that verse speaks to who our partner is or how God sees them. Sometimes an image comes to mind with an interpretation as to how it relates to our partner – "I saw a boat with its sail fully furled and I believe that God is saying that he sees you as a willing vessel with your whole being, wide open – ready to catch the wind of his Spirit and go wherever he leads you."

Sometimes the words of a song come to mind or a few short phrases that God wants to use as an encouragement for others. Sometimes we are reminded of an act of service we have seen our partner perform and how that was an encouragement to us and others.

And sometimes nothing comes to mind.

After the silence the partners turn to each other and share what they sensed God saying to them.

For those who didn't sense God giving them anything to share, I suggest that they just encourage their partner with what they already know about them – "I love your smile!" Sometimes, as they begin to encourage others – even when they didn't sense God saying anything specific – God begins to give them additional, encouraging information as they speak.

Even when something supernatural doesn't happen, people still receive encouragement – even from a simple heartfelt encouragement: "I think your voice is a wonderful gift that I see you using to glorify God. Thank you!"

Although I don't generally participate with the students on this exercise sometimes there is a shortage of people to make up the pairs and so I will link up with one of the students. One student I participated with in this exercise received significant insight from the Lord regarding things that he had been sharing with me through Lila Weber, my intercessor, over the previous year. Shelly spoke to me of the Lord wanting to encourage me to take time to be alone with him – not for preparation for a ministry trip – just a time alone with Jesus; time for him to build me up and refresh me anew. And also that God would provide for me a mentor – someone who I could receive from as opposed to someone else who I would need to give to. That was also something that I have been longing for over the past number of years.

What an encouraging (and convicting) reminder from a Lord who loves us and doesn't forget his promises or his instructions!

As I turned to share what God had put on my heart for her I breathed a silent cry, "Help me, Lord! I don't know where to take this!"

What the Lord had spoken to my heart in that time of silence was only, "Sarah laughed." I considered this to be only in reference to the fact that this young woman had been laughing at something earlier during the teaching session, and therefore, I was just thinking of that incidence and coming up with a scriptural reference for laughter – rather than anything that God might have been speaking to me. And because her name was Shelly, the 'Sarah laughed – Shelly laughed' comparison seemed to be merely coincidental.

As I attempted to hear something else, God just made those two words stick all the more and began to add some additional thoughts. I really knew nothing about Shelly other than the place she called home and that she was married to Ben. So as I turned to share with her I said, "I might be completely out in left field on this. Please forgive me if I am, but . . ." I said that I didn't really know anything about her and her husband or what their situation was but I felt that the words "Sarah laughed" had something to do with infertility. I felt that something had happened to cause infertility, like an accident or injury to her womb, but that she should not laugh at God's ability to bring a child into their lives. God wanted to provide a child for them. Whether to open up a dead womb, as in Sarah's case in the Bible, or to heal an injured, infertile womb, or to provide a child for them by another means – nothing was out of the realm of possibility for God. So she shouldn't laugh at the healing and the child that God wanted to provide for them. Rather, trust in God's ability.

After saying all this I apologetically said, "If this was way off the mark, please forgive me!" She then told me a bit of her story. Here are her words:

Being a practicing drug addict I had put myself in unhealthy places. One evening I went alone to a hotel to buy drugs. The two men inside the room offered me a drink and some drugs. With in an hour they had beaten me, raped me and left me for dead. I went to my car with half my torn clothes on. I had cried so much that I had no more tears left. I fell into my car shaking, moaning, in pain and an overwhelming feeling of wanting to die. I could not believe I let this happen. I was so tough and strong, what happened?

I drove to my father's house. I stayed in my room for about four days. I told my Dad and his new wife I was ill. I snuck out of my room to go to the bathroom and cleaned my wounds. I felt a filthiness that a shower could never clean. I was ashamed and embarrassed for what had happened to me. I didn't want anyone to know how stupid I was, or that this all started because I wanted to use drugs.

A week later I went to a clinic. I was physically ill and needed medical attention. After the doctor examined me, she knew I had been raped. She then told me I was pregnant. I was devastated. These men didn't just steal purity away from me, I felt as if they put the devil inside me as well. I was raised a Catholic, but as my family split, I split from the church. The nurse gave me three pamphlets of options: birth, adoption, or abortion. I picked abortion without hesitation. I had the abortion performed on Halloween night. After that night I thought the past was the past and I would never need to confront that pain again.

Shortly after that I went to my third drug treatment center. That was in December 1992, I have been clean since. Recovery from addiction was the door that helped me to seek God. I was seeking a spiritual way of life. In my first five years clean I became a productive member of society. I was successful in just about everything I did. I believed in God and even believed that Jesus was God's son. But there were other things I believed as well. One was that God could never forgive a girl that would kill a baby. I thought I was unforgivable.

I had one real relationship with a man before I was raped. After the men raped me any personal relations I had always ended in "let's be friends." I was scared, I felt damaged and I never wanted anyone to know what evil had happen to me or what evil I had done. On the outside I was functioning as a mature, successful young lady. However, I suffered from nightmares and flashbacks: seeing blood, hearing my own voice yelling, "Stop, stop!" Every Halloween after having the abortion I dreaded the day. I feared the memories and nightmares of this hellish anniversary.

Many years later I went out with a big group of friends for dinner. I met a gentleman named Ben. Ben made me laugh from the minute I met him to the time we all said our goodbyes that evening. I hadn't laughed like that in years. Ben started to heal my heart through laughter. He invited me to join him on different outings and we had lots of fun together. After a year of non-stop laughing Ben asked me to marry him and I accepted.

Neither of us had any kind of healthy example of marriage. We both knew we wanted to be married by a pastor. We also knew without God in our marriage were hopeless. Within three weeks of our engagement we were in pre-marriage counselling with the pastor of a church we really liked. Within months both Ben and I accepted Jesus as our Lord and Saviour. I shared with Ben my whole past and he assured me that his love for me didn't change.

We were married on May 20th, 2000. We talked about married life with kids. We also discussed if we didn't have children of our own then we would adopt. I secretly thought that I was damaged when raped and/or when I had the abortion. I felt that God might punish me for having an abortion. I kept these secrets to myself and tried to believe that our God is a good God.

Within a year we were full members of our church, serving wherever we could. By the next year the Lord called us on missions. Ben and I, with direction, felt that a short-term (nine months) mission trip was a good place to start. We sold anything we felt we could live without for support monies. We sold my car, quit our jobs, put education on hold and rented our home out.

We went to the training phase of our mission. It was two months long and in that time many speakers came. One morning in my personal prayer and mediation the Lord told me to tell two of the women leaders in confidence about my past and ask them to pray with me for healing. The next day the Lord put these women in my path and we prayed to the Lord. Then he revealed a vision to me:

As I lay on an alter Jesus was pouring water all over me. He was cleansing me. I heard the words, "You don't have to ask for forgiveness for the evil that was done to you my child." I left that prayer meeting knowing that the Lord was beginning to heal me.

A few days later a speaker came to our training time speaking about worship and prophetic encouragement. Later that evening we broke into small groups. I didn't have a partner so Gareth, the instructor, paired up with me. He gave the group a few more instructions and then we prayed and sat in silence. Then he lifted his head and said:

"I hear 'Sarah laughed' – like Sarah in the Bible doubting that she was going to have a son" (Genesis 18:10-15). "I feel like I need to tell you, Shelly, your womb is healed. Does any of this mean anything to you?"

I laughed to myself and thought, now? I am 35 years old, my husband and I have been trying for almost four years to have a baby. We had even started to look into adoption agencies. Another part of me was crying "Oh, please, Lord, let it be true." Gareth and I shared a little bit more that evening and I told him I was in a huge healing place right now with my past. Ben and I were wondering why we hadn't had children yet. I introduced Gareth to Ben and we promised to stay in touch.

The next weekend I went on a three day silent retreat. At the retreat the main facilitator was one of the women I prayed with a week before, halfway through the retreat I met with her about what God was saying to me in the silence. We went for a walk outside down a beautiful path.

I confessed to her the night before I awoke laughing hysterically, so loud that I woke all the women in my room. They couldn't yell at me because we were at a silent retreat. I privately thought that it was Sarah's laugh again. The facilitator also asked me if there was anything more revealed to me about the vision I had.

I told her it was so real, I could feel the water touching my inner soul: I could see myself getting buckets and buckets of water poured over me by Jesus. He was cleaning me from the guilt, shame and acts of the past. It wasn't one second later that it started to rain and pour a cleansing rain all over me.

The Lord wanted to make sure I was hearing him. He obviously wanted my attention: the prayers, visions, Gareth's prophetic words, the laughter and the rain, what was next?

Needless to say I was blown away! And fearful! What if God never healed her womb? But on reflection, the word wasn't that God would heal the womb but rather that God was able to heal and supply what she and her husband longed for – a child. I believe that God can open up dead wombs as he did in Sarah's case – as he has done in another friend's case.

And this young woman? She was immensely encouraged. It demonstrated to her that God had not forgotten about them! God cared for the yearning of her and her husband's hearts to be able to have children. Whether that will be through adoption or through pregnancy – both would be seen as God's provision.

Five months later, I received an email updating me about her situation. The couple was expecting their first child! Hallelujah!

Why did Paul say that he desired that everyone in the church would prophecy (1 Corinthians 14:5)? Prophetic encouragement builds up the body, encourages and strengthens the body. And it honours the Lord. It blesses *him* to have his people strengthen and encourage each other. It's a part of how we can walk-out our worship in the church and in society.

What would the church look like today if each believer would spend a few moments each week offering themselves to God as a vessel through which he could extend a word of encouragement, strengthening, or building? It would be a church that would reflect the grace and mercy of Jesus, a church that would worship God with abandon because they would continually hear God's voice through their Christian friends. Not only would they *receive* encouragement from others, they would *be* encouraged as God used them as his instrument of encouragement for others. And the world would notice how much we loved each other (John 13:35).

Here are some ideas to get you started in prophetic encouragement.

1. Start with a prayer asking God to bring to mind someone whom he would want you to encourage this week. Or God may have already been bringing someone to mind – perhaps for you to hold them up in prayer. Don't be afraid to speak those things that God gives you. You have little idea what is going on in another person's life. But God does!

2. Ask the Lord to bring something specific to mind that could be an encouragement for this individual. Don't try to be profound – don't try to come up with an awesome sounding 'word' that will make them realize how spiritual you are. That's a motivation mainly rooted in pride. The goal is not to have something great to say. The goal is to give God glory by encouraging someone by his Spirit's prompting.

   a. It might be a verse or two of Scripture. You might not even know what significance – if any – it has. If it is a word of encouragement from God for the other person it will be encouraging without any additional editorial comments.

   b. It may be Scripture with a bit of explanation that comes with it. If there is to be a bit of a commentary, interpretation or application to the Scripture that needs to be added, allow God to reveal it to you. Don't try and 'come up with' a plausible explanation just to fill out the encouragement.

   c. It may be a picture or mental image that represents something you know about the person and fits with that which would encourage them. Or it might not! Yet God can still use it to speak into the other person's life.

   d. It might be a song or poem that comes to mind.

   e. It may simply be an act or activity you witnessed them doing that God reminds you of as you pray.

3. Meet with the person face-to-face, call them on the phone, email or write a letter. Encouragement can come in a variety of ways.

4. Stay away from saying, "Thus saith the Lord!"

I believe it is better to be honest in your communication by saying something more along the lines of, "As I was asking God who he wanted me to encourage your name came to mind. And as I prayed for you God reminded me of (this or that)," or, "God brought to my mind this Scripture (picture, song, etc) which I believe he wants to use to encourage you today."

5. Pray for the person. Even if what you sensed God bringing to mind was completely wrong – or it didn't seem to connect in any way with the person – prayer is always something that will encourage. And that is the goal of the gift of prophecy – to encourage, build up and strengthen the body.

6. Love the people of God. Prophetic words are tricky in the church. There are many abuses that fall into the category of, "The Lord said." Words from the Lord are not your opinion. More often than not, the words you speak have little meaning to you. Too often we get confused with our role and the Holy Spirit's role. Our role is to simply obey. When God asks us to give a word to a fellow believer, we simply need to give that word. If he asks us to walk with that believer through a time of discipline, we need to walk with them. When we become judgmental, impatient, rude, angry, hateful, dissenting, we no longer have given the word in love. We may be right, but we are simply a very noisy interference to God's work. In the worst case scenario, we can actually block God's work when we don't operate with love.

Above all, we need to let the Holy Spirit do his work his way. I know that I need to get out of the way when God speaks so that others only see God and not me. Years ago, Esther, a young woman from another town visited our College & Career Bible study. When she left, Gayle said, totally out of the blue, "She is going to become Dave Corbett's wife." I laughed. She just shrugged and said, "Watch." Then she let it go. She didn't try to make it happen. She didn't say anything to anyone else. But she was right. And when the right time came, this prophetic word became an encouragement from God and confirmation of the relationship. And I had the joy of officiating at Dave and Esther's wedding a couple of years later!

7. Do it again. And again.

The crowd joined in the attack against Paul and Silas,
and the magistrates ordered them to be stripped and beaten.
After they had been severely flogged, they were thrown into prison,
and the jailer was commanded to guard them carefully.
Upon receiving such orders, he put them in the inner cell
and fastened their feet in the stocks.
About midnight Paul and Silas were praying and singing hymns to God,
and the other prisoners were listening to them.
Acts 16:22-25

CHAPTER NINETEEN

SUFFERING AND WORSHIP
Worshipping Jesus in the midst of adversity and trouble

I was sitting in a McDonald's restaurant when I overheard an interesting conversation at the next table. A middle-aged couple was in deep conversation with a young man about beginning a life with Jesus. As they talked, they described what it would mean to give his life to Jesus. I leaned into the conversation, curious to see where they were going with it.

They started by describing the redemptive work of Jesus, forgiving the young man of his sin and empowering him with the Holy Spirit so that he could live a different life. "Wow!" I thought, "God, in the midst of fast food!"

Then the conversation took a deep fork. The new path took a road that many of us mistakenly travel. The couple told the young man that life with

Christ meant the end of all his problems. You see, they were giving this young man a proposition statement that made Christianity very attractive. They explained that once we began a walk with Jesus, he would bless us and we would have everything we wanted. They said that, as a Christian, his relationship with his girlfriend would turn out (and of course, she would turn to Jesus!). With Jesus in his life, he would get a better job and his life would get on track.

Wow, I thought – who wouldn't want to follow Jesus! It's a guarantee for success – at least, as our society defines success!

I thought, "How small we have made Jesus." Perhaps we are so driven by marketing and presenting a palatable, seeker-friendly Jesus that we mess with the message. We rationalize Christianity in a Westernized version of individualism and commercialism. Sometimes I think we have lost the essence of salvation – that we have been saved from the power of evil, exchanging eternal life in hell for life everlasting with Jesus. For some unexplained reason, we are satisfied with a job promotion, a new car, a nice house, a beautiful girlfriend.

We are captivated by the immediate.

I have no doubt that the power of the Holy Spirit is there to lead and guide us, to instruct us in right living. He heals, restores and equips us. But coming to Jesus is not a solution for daily problems – a magical formula that makes everything smooth. Perhaps, if we truly followed Jesus with radical abandon, we would face much more difficult times.

Coming to Jesus is the height of paradox, a paradox that seems wrong in our world. Jesus asks us to give up our life so that we can win it back. I thought of that recently as I agonized at the number of broken relationships in the church. Some of them had good reasons to be broken. Promises had been broken, stupid mistakes made and often, there is a history of not dealing with issues. But Jesus asks us to give up our life – to lose what we think we desire, so that we can have all he desires for us.

Truly living as a passionate worshipper of God may lead to criticism, loss of friends, missing out on a deserved promotion. We may have to stand up and stand out, because our faith in Jesus means that we live by a different standard.

Following Jesus means following a pathway that is unexpected. I remember when I left my last pastoral position. It seemed to me that God was very clear in his expectation. He had asked me to leave the place I was ministering in and I was to move into a completely new direction. I left confident, looking forward to new success. But I had no idea what that was!

For five long months I prayed and begged God to give me a clue. You have to see this situation. Gayle had been staying home with the kids, doing some work marking papers for the University, but wasn't bringing in near enough to keep up with the payments. And, instead of working at whatever job I might have gotten to bring some money into our home, I was in a cold basement of a church – praying!

Friends, members of the church and even mature Christians didn't withhold their insight. They encouraged me to take any job that came my way so that my family would be cared for. But I truly believed that God called me to a period of rest and seeking. And it was immensely costly for me and my family. There have been long term financial repercussions – as the months without an adequate salary stretched into several years – even after I began the *Make Us Holy* ministries. It was truly a sacrifice.

Was it a mistake? No, I don't believe so.

Did it change the direction our lives were taking up to that point? There is no doubt.

Historically, radical Christians have made decisions that did not make sense to success-oriented friends and relatives. Look at Paul. First of all, Paul was a man with a logical mind and a sense of purposeful passion. He hated Christians and had spent a good deal of his professional life tracking down believers and persecuting them. Then, one day, on the road to Damascus, he was blinded by a light from heaven and Jesus confronted him. Man, that defied all logic. When the light rescinded he opened his eyes to find that he could not see. He was led to a home where he fasted and prayed for three days (Acts 9:1-9).

Next, the Lord sent Ananias, a believer living in Damascus, to go and lay hands on Paul (whose name still was Saul at the time) so that he might be filled with the power of the Holy Spirit to fulfill his calling (Acts 9:10-19).

And what was his calling? Well, God showed how much he was going to have to *suffer* for the sake of the name of Jesus (Acts 9:16). In just a short days of becoming a believer, Paul's life was dynamically and terrifyingly changed.

He had a high position in the church. He was educated and respected. I don't imagine many of his rabbi buddies were all that warm when he came to them to explain that God had called him to preach the Good News of Jesus Christ to the Gentiles! Following Jesus came at a high cost for Paul.

The apostle Peter warns new believers to be prepared for suffering.

> *Dear friends, do not be surprised at the painful trial you are suffering, as though something strange were happening to you. But rejoice that you participate in the sufferings of Christ, so that you may be overjoyed when his glory is revealed. If you are insulted because of the name of Christ, you are blessed, for the Spirit of glory and of God rests on you. If you suffer as a Christian, do not be ashamed, but praise God that you bear that name. (1 Peter 4:12-14,16)*

Jesus is not a one-step program to instant success. Western Christians today seem to believe that life with Jesus means success defined by worldly standards – a good job, a good family, a good reputation. God's blessings are evaluated in standards that God rejects: the amount of money we earn, the status of our position, the ease of gaining increased success. Testimonies seem to have a common theme – "life before Christ was filled with troubles, but when I accepted Jesus all my troubles went away."

Christ restores and renews our lives, gives us focus and purpose. And often times, because of that, our lives do become more deliberate and measured in discipline, energy and passion. But to define the Christian's walk in the context of Western comfort is rejecting the true and horrendous pain that millions of Christians face every day around the world.

When trials and suffering happen, we don't walk through them alone. We walk with One who holds us in our hour of deepest need. The challenge of living a life of worship is to worship God in the good and the bad – having his praise on our lips even when life sucks! Worshipping him even when we are suffering, in pain, or experiencing oppression, trial, or grief isn't easy, but it *is* necessary.

In early spring of 2004, I returned from a month of ministry in Guatemala and Belize. God was doing some awesome things in the lives of the students from the Outtatown Discipleship School (a program of the Canadian Mennonite University in Winnipeg, Manitoba, Canada <http://www.outtatown.com>). During my last week there, about 30 older adults came down with CMU's *Adventure for the Soul* tour – two weeks exploring Guatemala and interacting with a variety of ministries – discovering the awesome creation of God among different cultures. On a Sunday afternoon, halfway through their trip, the group was struck by a shockingly unexpected event. While swimming in the Pacific Ocean, a riptide swept about 10 participants off their feet. Three were caught in the tide. Only one escaped.

The experience of grief for the group was agonizing. For the spouses – it was an horrendous nightmare. There was a sense of disbelief – as if what had happened was just a bad dream and they would wake up in the morning and everything would be back to normal. As I sat with the spouses in a hotel room the evening before they flew home to Canada, I became incredibly aware of my inability to comfort – the lack of adequate vocabulary to console. And yet, I also felt the power of God to accomplish what I couldn't for these two grieving people as they looked to him for strength that wasn't in them – or me – to give.

Suffering, loss and pain are a reality. When we experience suffering, either because of personal loss or persecution – worship takes on a different dimension. Our laments and complaints draw us back to the arms of the Father who holds us and comforts us. There we experience the strength of having suffered – in a small way – as our Saviour has suffered. And again – in a small way – receiving the indescribable comfort that he also received. Our worship miraculously enables us to praise in spite of our pain. Our suffering and pain miraculously gives us the ability to stand alongside others in pain and suffering and help them to worship – to know the comfort of a God of all comforts.

> *All praise to the God and Father of our Lord Jesus Christ. He is the source of every mercy and the God who comforts us. He comforts us in all our troubles so that we can comfort others. When others are troubled, we will be able to give them the same comfort God has given us. You can be sure that the more we suffer for Christ, the more God will shower us with his comfort through Christ.*
> *(2 Corinthians 1:3-5 – NLT)*

Our North American experience of Christianity is not the norm. Hundreds of thousands of believers in other countries face the possibility of death each day. Many live in countries so poor, that their daily existence is totally dependent on the grace of God. In many other parts of the world, living the Christian life means sacrifice, giving up, persecution and even death. Few evangelists use an altar call that says: "Come accept Jesus and he'll ask you to die in service for him. Who will answer his call?" We are much more likely to soften the call. We rarely talk about losing our life so that God's work can be done. But that's what God asks us. He asks us to let go of our right for life, so that he can accomplish much more in us.

Several years ago I spoke at a youth retreat. The youth pastor told me that there were a number of kids coming who had been attending the youth group but had never responded to an invitation to invite Jesus to be a part of their lives. They all enjoyed going to the youth group but never responded to an opportunity to give their lives to Jesus Christ. He asked me if I would give an opportunity for people to accept Jesus following one of my talks.

On a Saturday night I spoke of biblical and historical characters who answered God's call of salvation and gave up their lives to serve him, some in terrible circumstances, others in literally giving their lives in death. I then shared stories of Christians throughout history and today who gave themselves to God fully and who suffered greatly to be found worthy of that calling.

Following the talk I gave the teens an opportunity to invite Jesus into their lives, stressing that life would not necessarily become easier. It might even become more difficult because everyday they would have to choose to die to themselves and live for Jesus. And it might also mean that God would call them to serve him in a way that could, quite literally, cause their deaths. Then I asked, "If you are willing to say 'yes' to Jesus, even if it may mean that you will die for carrying his name, put up your hand."

I wasn't expecting anyone to respond. It wasn't exactly a feel-good altar call. I wasn't promising them anything that was overtly successful or attractive. I was calling them to die. I could have toned the message down and made it easy to respond – letting them find out the truth of a call to follow Jesus as they were discipled – but I felt that wouldn't be truthful to what I felt God wanting me to say.

Five young people responded. The youth pastor was overwhelmed and perplexed because it wasn't a message that made it easy to want to become a Christian. As he prayed and spoke with the students he found that the reason they wanted to commit their lives to Jesus was because it was something worth giving their life for. Anything less was really no different than what their lives already were. They already had 'the good life'. What they wanted was something worth living for because it was something worth dying for.

That stunned me. I was struck by how many times I resist challenging myself and others to live a life that is radically different from others in our world. These kids were so right. Why would they follow a God that only gave them more of the stuff they already had? They were yearning for a God that had the power to impact the world. They wanted the opportunity to commit their lives to a life that was dynamic, life-challenging and world-changing.

Believers throughout the ages have encountered more difficulties after their conversions than before they came to Christ. Hebrew 11 lists many people who lived by faith even though, when they died, they still had not received the promise of that faith. In spite of their trials and suffering they continued to live by faith (Hebrews11:13). The life of the Anabaptists in the early 1500's is another example of costly Christianity. Living for Christ did not mean the absence of trials or suffering in life then and it still doesn't today.

In Foxe's *Book of Martyrs* are many stories of people whose life of praise and worship to God in the midst of persecution and death caused many to turn and worship Jesus. One story tells about the martyrdom of Faustines and Jovita who were brothers and citizens of Brescia, Italy.

Foxe writes:

> *Their torments were so many, and their patience so great, that*
> *Calocerius, a pagan, beholding them, was struck with admiration, and*
> *exclaimed in a kind of ecstasy, 'Great is the God of the Christians!'*
> *For which he was apprehended, and suffered a similar fate*
> (John Foxe. *Foxe's Book of Martyrs*. Online posting.
> The Third Persecution, Under Trajan, A.D. 108. 16 Oct. 2004.
> <http://www.connecticut-adventist.org/Bible_Study/Foxe/Foxe_2.3.htm>).

Sammy Tippit said:

> *Christianity is the glory and grace of God in the heart of the hurting*
> *believer. A Christian receives no exemption from the hurts of*
> *humanity. It's often in the midst of suffering that the Christian learns*
> *to worship Jesus Christ. He learns to appreciate and adore Him as he*
> *gains a greater understanding of Christ's suffering. It's in the trying*
> *circumstances that his understanding of God's love is deepened*
> (Sammy Tippit. 'Suffering and Worship.' Online posting. Sammy
> Tippit Ministries: God's Love in Action. 16 Oct. 2004.
> <http://www.gospelcom.net/glia/2001/wow/st_032601.shtml>).

We have a young woman in our congregation who left her home, her husband and young daughter to save the lives of herself and her unborn infant. She doesn't even know if they are still alive. She knows that they live in a land where war and conflict threatens lives everyday. When I hear her pray in her mother tongue, I can't understand a word – but I understand this: this young woman, throughout her trials and suffering, trusts God implicitly. She is grateful for her life and the life of her child. She has nothing in this new country, but she is making it her home – and she counts herself as rich!

I admit that my own worship in the midst of suffering or persecution has been limited. But I sense that our easy North American Christian life is about to get shaken up. Our 'Christian countries' are losing their affinity to Christ's values. A person from the former Soviet Union was asked to comment on his perspectives of North American Society over against the regimes of Communism under which he grew up. He responded that it was frightening to see North American society rushing madly into the same abyss that Russia is now trying to crawl out of – a life without God.

In a sense we are always bound to repeat history. And the church throughout history has gone from a persecuted church to a stabilizing force in society and then to complacency and irrelevance. I struggle to worship in a way that will dynamically impact my community in a relevant, life-giving way.

Our time of freedom of expression and worship is coming to an end – even in our tolerant society. Because the one thing tolerant societies cannot stand are absolutes. Jesus said, "I am the way, the truth and the life. *No one* comes to the Father except through me" (John 14:6 – emphasis mine).

While studying Spanish in Guatemala in 2002, I spent a fair amount of time with the students. Each week and most weekends we would go on short sightseeing tours in and around the city of Quezaltenango. We took in the variety of cultural and religious diversity that the country had to offer. When we had a Mayan priestess perform the Mayan new year ceremony, all the students wanted to participate and offer up their prayers to the Mayan gods and have the priestess offer a blessing for them. When we visited the temple of patron saint, Maximon (or San Simón), the students were anxious to offer a prayer request to San Simón for wealth or relationships or peace or other things represented by lighting a different coloured candle.

But once, when we were coming into the town of Chichicastenango we saw an evangelical church group singing praise songs and giving testimonies in the market square. The students I was with immediately began to criticize and mock the group.

Later that evening I confronted them. I found it ironic that they were so tolerant of pagan gods – eager to participate in the rituals and ceremonies that they represented. At first, I couldn't understand why they were blatantly intolerant to this evangelical group. But Christianity was way too close to them. They knew a lot about the church. They couldn't rationalize accepting a tradition that came from abuse. They pointed out a series of really bad moments in Christian history; everything from the Crusades of the 11th to 13th centuries, to televangelism, to the suppression of women's rights, to the use of corporal punishment for children. Many gave personal examples of how the church had clearly played the game of religion. Although they were very tolerant of all different religious expressions, they were not tolerant of Christians or Christianity.

If they had given all the bad examples found within Jewish history they would have been called anti-Semitic, or of a Muslim culture and religion – and many similar examples can be found in each – they would have been called anti-Muslim racists. But Christianity is fair game. Our society is becoming more and more tolerant of everything *except* Christianity. And I think that trend will grow.

When they were done I asked them, "So is that how you feel about me? I have given my life to follow Jesus and I am willing to die for him. Yet you reduce my faith down to a handful of bad examples without ever looking at what lies beneath – in the same willingness that you've demonstrated for other religions."

They all knew that I was a pastor. And they remained quiet for a moment before saying, "No, we don't see you that way. You don't fit the mould." I responded, "Perhaps it's because you have taken time to get to know me that has altered your opinion. Don't you think that perhaps you need to give yourself the opportunity to get to know other Christians as well?"

They remained silent.

You know, these young adults were very willing to dip into things that required nothing from them. It was fun. Their tolerance of other cultures and religions was really little more than 'play' to them. None of them were willing to commit their lives to a belief system or devote themselves to serving a god – any god! They were just sampling – like we sample new food items at the grocery store.

That winter, I was impressed more and more at the attitude of Western people. At a time when a hunger for spirituality is at an all-time high, people who live a life of a true worshipper are at an all time low. Our young people are seeking spiritual insight from many different sources, often mixing several spiritual traditions and religions together. There is little affinity for the believer that there is truth. A friend recently asked me what I thought of a quote that suggested that truth was always changing. Yeah, that statement flies in the face of the truth statements Christians have hung on to. But I challenged her. What is truth? Do we say when our perceptions change, that truth is changing?

We have been severely misled to understand that we can know God's truth in completeness. 1 Corinthians 13:12 tells us that until we see Jesus, we only see things in part. We will not know truth fully until we see God. That doesn't mean that God isn't true – it simply means that the truth of God is so broad and expansive that even in all of our lifetime we will not completely grasp the fullness of it.

We need to begin to tell the story of God and the Good News of Jesus with boldness – even though people will not accept it. We are responsible for the people who have not met Jesus if we have kept the message to ourselves.

Today, we have the freedom to speak. We live in a world where terrorism, mental illness, broken relationships, are messing with people's lives. We serve a God that is beyond our own weakness. We serve a God, that even when the things in our world fall apart, is in total control. Do we believe that enough to live like it?

When suffering, persecution, trials of all kinds come – will we be found as a people who worship Jesus in the midst of them? Or will we deny him? God calls us to worship him at all times. I believe that when suffering and persecution come, those who have developed a longing to be walking worshippers – people pursuing intimacy with their God in every circumstance of their daily lives – will find strength, comfort and rest in God.

Normally I end each chapter with a few steps to grow in learning how better to worship God in the particular focus of the section. But how do I provide steps for worshipping God in suffering? Perhaps these few steps are not too trivial to be helpful for I sense that as you do go through trials and suffering, God's Spirit will guide you to the places you need to go to be comforted and encouraged. Steps 1–3 are taken from a website article (Dennis Rupert. 'Eight Explanations for Suffering Found in the Bible.' Online posting. New Life Community Church. 16 Oct. 2004. <http://www.new-life.net/sufferng.htm>).

1. Suffering is real. Some religions (such as Hinduism, Christian Science) believe that suffering is just illusion. But the pain, grief, and sorrow that we experience in this life is not imaginary. It is real. We cannot talk about suffering in some detached theological manner. Anguish, distress, torment, and agony cannot be reasoned away by some appeal to a few Scriptures taken out of context. Suffering was so real that Jesus himself came to live in it, experience the full depth of it, conquer it, and redeem it. His suffering was real. So is ours.

2. Suffering came into the world as a result of the fall of humanity. – Death, pain, grief, loneliness, persecution, rejection and all other

types of suffering were not part of God's original world (Genesis 1:31; 3:17-19; 5:29; Romans 5:12,14,18; 8:20-22; 1 Corinthians 15:21-22; Revelation 21:3-4). God is not the author for all the bad things that happen in the world. We, all of humanity, prove ourselves to be children of Adam as we follow our sinful desires instead of following Jesus. We are the ones to blame for the curse that the world is under.

3. God is in control and sovereign over all events. – Suffering is real, but it is not the only reality. There is more to life than pain. God is in charge and nothing happens apart from his knowledge or involvement at some level (Deuteronomy 32:39; 1 Samuel 2:6-9; 1 Chronicles 29:11-12; Proverbs 16:4; Job 2:9-10; Ecclesiastes 9:1; Isaiah 45:7; Jeremiah 18:1-23; Lamentations 3:37-38; Daniel 2:20-21; 4:17,25,35; Matthew 10:29; Luke 1:53; Acts 1:7; 17:24-26,28; Ephesians 1:4-5; Colossians 1:17; Revelation 4:11). God will use and is using the suffering of this world for his own purposes.

4. Read the biblical texts that speak of the suffering servant (Isaiah 40-55). We have not yet suffered to the extent that our Lord Jesus has suffered. Yes, our suffering is real but there is one who suffered for us. He knows our pain. He will help us to bear it and carry us through it.

5. Prepare for persecution without inviting it.

I try never to give a non-believing person a good reason to hate me for what I believe. So when I share my faith with people I try to use words that open up understanding rather than cloaking it in religious terms. People deserve to hear a testimony of your relationship with Jesus in a way that can help them to understand it clearly.

Now I want to tell you, dear brothers and sisters,
what God in his kindness has done for the churches in Macedonia.
Though they have been going through much trouble and hard times,
their wonderful joy and deep poverty have overflowed in rich generosity.
For I can testify that they gave not only what they could afford but far more.
And they did it of their own free will. They begged us again and again for the
gracious privilege of sharing in the gift for the Christians in Jerusalem.
Best of all, they went beyond our highest hopes, for their first action was to dedicate
themselves to the Lord and to us for whatever directions God might give them.
So we have urged Titus, who encouraged your giving in the first place, to return
to you and encourage you to complete your share in this ministry of giving.
2 Corinthians 8:1-6

CHAPTER TWENTY

JOYFUL GIVING

An expression of worship

My ministry is a faith ministry. Very kind and generous people share their resources with us and enable the ministry to be carried out. I am grateful for their response to God's call in their lives to give. I am also immensely humbled by their generosity.

But sometimes, the everyday gets in the way of my confidence in God. Yeah, I know that God is trustworthy. I know that, like the birds in the sky and the flowers in the field, God will provide everything that my family needs (note: that is 'needs', not wants). Yet some days I take a quick look at the bank statement and gasp. There are times when I am tempted to believe that God doesn't really care. But then I have to sit back and think . . . how has God provided our needs?

WORSHIP WALK

Let me tell you a short story.

We were ending our three years of ministry in the central British Columbia town of Williams Lake. In about a month we would be heading out across the country to Kitchener, Ontario. Our passion for ministry had grown in our three years there at Cariboo Bethel Church and we were anxious about what this new chapter of God's leading would bring. We knew that his call was clear but had only the outline of what he wanted to accomplish in and through us in Kitchener.

Our family was growing up. Our two boys, Chris and Dan – then ten and eight years old – were stretching into their pre-teen years and our daughter, Carine – then four years old – was as active and animated as ever.

We had a slight problem. Leaving the farm and going to seminary had shattered our financial plans. Going to seminary for two years didn't help strengthen our financial position. Nor did our Associate Pastor salary!

We needed a new car. We were driving a little Honda Civic. Carine, outspoken even at age four, made it crystal clear that she was not about to sit under a guitar and cramped between her two brothers all the way to Ontario. The car was just too small to pack the family and all the things we needed to take on a cross-Canada trek.

We had looked around and no matter how we did the numbers, they weren't really working for us. We began to pray that God would provide suitable transportation for us before we needed to leave. We sold the Honda and for a couple of months were a single motorcycle family! The moving date was closing in and so we enlisted the prayers of a few prayer warriors to help bend the ear of God for this urgent request.

Then God surprised us.

We were sitting in the Dairy Queen with a very good friend, Dave Corbett (note: the same young man who would fall in love and marry Esther - see chapter eighteen). Dave had just bought a brand new Mazda 626. He had slid his keys over the table to us saying that God had asked him to give us his car! Not sell us his car or loan us his car – but give us his car. And there were his keys lying in front of us on the table. "Take them. The car is yours."

WOW! We were stunned.

But here's lesson 1 . . . . To celebrate the generosity and blessing of God, one must swallow middle class, suburban logic and be willing to accept the gift God gives in the way he gives it.

So we thanked Dave profusely and gave him back his keys. To this day we still feel that we had slapped God and God's friend in the face. We were too proud and too faithless to trust that if God had told his son to give away his new car that he would actually provide something else.

So our journey continued . . .

Five years later, God called us out of youth ministry to follow him into what eventually became *Make Us Holy* ministries. But in the five months of waiting upon God for clear direction as to 'what' he was calling us to follow him in, I had no job, no income – only a word from God to be patient, to wait and not to worry. We had just purchased a home eight months earlier. Gayle was working part time as a Teaching Assistant at the University of Waterloo. She brought in enough money for food and a few small extras each month. I had no idea about where the mortgage payments would come from – let alone taxes, upkeep and repairs.

One week into my time of unemployment we received a phone call from another friend out west. We had not spoken with her for several years. 'Ann' said that God had prompted her to reconnect with us. I told her that I knew

God was preparing me for something but not knowing what that was as yet, only that I was to be patient, to wait and not to worry. She promised to be praying together with us as we waited on God's direction.

A week later we received a letter from her. In it she wrote that as she prayed about what her part was in all this, she felt God asking her to supply our mortgage payments for one year. In the envelope were 12 post-dated cheques – each enough to cover for the amount of the mortgage, property tax and insurance.

I recently asked Ann to write a response about the story behind her gift. She responded through an email which I am enclosing here.

In terms of what was going on in my life at the time, I would have to say that the Lord was very busy renewing my own heart and mind. At that time in my life, he chose to reveal himself to me in many way, but most of all, he revealed his love for me in ways that I had not understood previously. The Lord revealed so much of his love, heart and thoughts to me that it was as if earthly priorities disappeared and I could only see the Lord and the things that would matter to him. While it was an intense period in my relation to the Lord, in general the things he revealed to me at that time have become constants in my life. It was as if he renewed my mind to, think like he thinks and to see the priorities he does. Of course there is always a long way to go in anyone's life, but in general that period of time in my life turned out to be one of significant permanent change.

So in some ways, the above leads into my reasons for being able to give sacrificially. When one is consumed with the Lord's priorities, one's energies, focus and decisions become pointed in those directions. So when you spoke to me about the time of transition in your own life and I thought about what the Lord was doing in mine, it felt clear to me that the Lord was nudging me to support you in your endeavour. It didn't seem like a huge revelation, but rather, just the obvious next thing to do. I also discovered that he gives you the faith to believe that you can fulfill a commitment that requires you to give sacrificially. (Interestingly enough, Revenue Canada contacted me the next year and required that I submit original receipts of my giving – I'm sure they were suspicious of my charitable giving claims.) For me this commitment actually necessitated altering my living situation for a period of time, choosing a room and board situation instead of just my own place, but the Lord also blessed and used that in my life.

In the end, what has been the impact on me? Most testimonies I have heard about giving, seem to include some description of major financial blessing from the Lord. I can't think of any particular significant financial blessing I received after that time, though I have always had more than enough, wonderful job opportunities and I cannot say that I have ever really lacked. In your letter you implied that maybe getting married was God's gift to me. I think that it was, though I've never really thought about it in terms of it being a response to giving.

Rather, my own thoughts on the topic are, that the real blessings are the constant companionship of the Lord himself, the counsel and teaching of the Holy Spirit, the ability to have hope and joy and peace in a very challenging world, the ability to be a solid, stable human being with ability to contribute meaningfully in many ways, rather than being dependent and drawing off of the resources of others. I think that the Lord would have given those things to me, whether I had given sacrificially that particular time or not. But I have come to think, that when as humans, we become completely taken up with the Lord and his priorities, to the point that it impacts our decisions, wallets etc, that he takes you to a place of intimacy with himself and that the other things in life really matter very little.

Life will have its ups and downs, but the ups and downs have less ability to disturb you, because the power of God is a stronger force in your life than what is going on around you.

So the intimacy with God is the real, and maybe only, blessing. Nothing else compares with the times you hear him tell you something new about himself, about your own life, or about what his purposes for something are. Nothing else compares with sitting in his presence. Nothing else compares with considering his love and grace to a hurting world. Nothing else compares to salvation, living in the lightness of being forgiven, the constant works of healing he does in you life and the purpose he, and only he, can give to your life. Nothing else compares to the constant fellowship of the Spirit.

In simplicity, though I know that he gives many physical blessings, I would never want to elevate them to the height of having an ongoing and constant relationship with him. Knowing the Lord makes you feel lucky to be alive and amazed to find yourself having a small part in the things he is doing. He inspires passion to know him more, to be continuously more and more rid of my old nature and to be a servant.

Lesson 2 . . . . God does not turn away. He gives us another chance to test his ability to care for us. And he does it unexpectedly – in ways we can never imagine on our own, who or how or when he will act.

This time, we were faithful. We have no way of knowing how God has blessed her for her generosity. I think she is bang on in her response to me: our blessing is intimacy with God. Her blessing is the growth and constancy of that intimacy. For both of us, this experience is one more moment on the journey of knowing God better.

Since starting *Make Us Holy* ministries I have had two guitars given to me through several people's monetary donations. Each one was given by people who were not financially well-off. But each one gave because they knew that they were being asked by God to do what, humanly speaking, was a foolish thing to do.

A third guitar was given by a friend who, in response to God's prompting, gave me his own dearly loved guitar. The guitar I had been using for several years began to develop electronic problems. After a half dozen times at the repair shop failed to correct the pickup problems, I began to cry out to God for his help. We didn't have the funds to purchase a new guitar and I had a major conference coming up in which I desperately needed a dependable guitar. Three days after calling out to God a friend of mine showed up at my door with his guitar. He had only recently received this guitar and said he just wanted to show it to me and get my opinion as to its value. After examining it I realized that it was a very well made, easy to play instrument. He responded, "So you like it?" I told him that I did and he handed it to me and said, "It's yours!"

He said that three days earlier as he had been waiting upon God in prayer, God had told him to give his guitar to me. He had fought with God for three days before obeying – because he really loved that guitar. A few years earlier he had lost his job, his car, his home and had to depend on social assistance for a time. In those years God taught him about trusting him for everything. Now, as they were beginning to get their lives back together, he realized that he never again wanted to hold onto things God was asking him to let go.

For two years, until God asked me to return the guitar, every time I played it I was reminded of the incredible way that God supplies our needs – sometimes from those who are most needy. It is a humbling thing to be the recipient of people's generosity – especially when it comes in the form of a gift that is too great for them to afford to give.

Lesson 3 . . . . Possessions, property and money, 'things,' have no value or ownership in God's family. They are to be used to their maximum benefit for the glory of God.

When I read Paul's description of the generosity of the Macedonians in 2 Corinthians 8:1-6, I begin to get a glimpse of how a worshipper gives extravagantly to the work of the Kingdom of God. Giving is an act of worship – especially when we are asked to give beyond reason, a true sacrifice of praise.

Three gifts were given generously by the Macedonians. They gave themselves to God – daring God to use them in dynamic ways. Then they gave themselves to Paul and Titus – they offered to partner with Paul and Titus in their missionary vision in whatever way they required. Finally they gave a cash gift to be used in support of the Christians in Jerusalem. The Message says it wonderfully:

> *This was totally spontaneous, entirely their own idea, and caught us completely off guard. What explains it was that they had first given themselves unreservedly to God and to us. The other giving simply flowed out of the purposes of God working in their lives.*
> *(2 Corinthians 8:5 – Msg)*

A worshipper will always find a way to give.

First, worshippers offer themselves to God. This is not a one time thing. It is an offering of gratitude in gratefulness, for the cost of our salvation. It places us smack in the middle of overwhelming grace that has given us life. This is a primary act of worship – an act of giving. Jesus asks us each day to take up our cross daily and follow him (Luke 9:23). Our serving and giving to others is secondary to the initial act of willingness to give our lives to God.

Second, worshippers offer themselves to others in service for the kingdom. This fits into God's plan of kingdom and community. God's children are not independent. They work together in multiple roles to fulfill the mission and purpose of God in this world. It's the ultimate body principle. We are willing to work alongside as a team.

Sometimes we lose ourselves in the spiritual mindset of service. We mentally and emotionally articulate a willingness to give everything and wait for God to tell us what we are supposed to do. We forget that God simply expects obedience – that means our hands and our feet enact what our mind and heart know. While that seems simplistic – it's tough. We 'know' a lot more than we do.

Service may not be a big thing – it might simply be taking the time to care about someone by listening to their story, by sharing a meal with them, by giving them encouragement during a down time. But it means that we always think about the needs of others before our own needs.

Third, worshippers offer gifts of resources that help others. The distribution of wealth is not and never has been equal. People in our churches and our communities have different levels of wealth. Our purpose on earth is not to collect treasures – for the treasures we collect will quickly confirm where our heart is. There are many stories of how people have responded to a need of another person or group even though their own need was great. And God, somehow, was able to provide for the deficit in miraculous ways. There is something miraculous that happens when we give, even in our own need.

One more story – it's short.

In the early days of our youth ministry in Kitchener we were asked to host a mission team of 13 young people over a weekend. That meant feeding them. Our finances were really low – in fact, we didn't have any extra cash – period! We knew it was the right thing to do to have these young people in the house – we just weren't quite sure how God would provide the extra food we needed.

On Friday morning, just before Gayle went out to shop, she checked the mailbox. There was an envelope with more than enough cash to cover the food costs for the weekend. It was anonymous – without even a note. We hadn't told anyone that we needed food that weekend. But God provided!

It's still hard for me to totally trust God – even as I tell the stories of his faithfulness, I wonder how *Make Us Holy* will meet its budget. I wonder how we can grow and move into new areas. After all I have received from him I still find myself becoming concerned with his ability to provide!

Let me remind you of one more lesson . . . . God knows our needs and promises that he will care for us.

Let me digress once more to the stunning offer of that Mazda 626 I mentioned at the beginning of this chapter. Frankly, I was too embarrassed to take that gift. How would we explain such an extravagant gift to others in the church? How would our friend Dave explain to the bank, which had loaned him money for the car, that the car he was paying off was licensed and being driven by someone else in another province? What kind of a dead-beat provider was I that I couldn't supply a car for my own family by our own means?

I asked Dave, recently, to reflect on why he was willing to give such an extravagant gift. He responded through an email which I am enclosing here:

My heart at that time was very hungry to obey Jesus in whatever was happening and hungry to see God's provision in giving. I had just bought the car and thought it was a good investment and dedicated it to the Lord, a lesson God taught me from an earlier vehicle (which is another story). In rejoicing in the new car I also knew the great blessing I had in this new car, many others did not have. With that in mind I felt God's heart was "as freely as I received, freely I should be willing to give" (Matthew 10:8b).

As far as offering it to you that night, the simplicity of the phase: "If you see someone in need and do not help them how can the Love of God be in you," (1 John 3:17) was in my mind. I don't remember there being much forethought just that it was the right thing to do. How would God work it out? I had no idea. I had some nervousness but I was up for the adventure. I must add, it would be hard do describe the amount of overwhelming love and appreciation I had for you two. Giving such a gift to you was not a difficult thing.

What happened subsequent to you not receiving my car as a gift? I probably thought, "Praise the Lord! I don't have to explain to my Dad where my new car is!" As spiritual as we are we still fight fear of our parents! I enjoyed the blessing of that vehicle for a number of years. I believe God's blessing was on that vehicle, I drove it over 200,000 km with little to no repairs and no accidents. I sold it cheaply to friends in need six years later and they just sold it in the spring (16 years old now) with over 350,000 km and still running good. I want that kind of blessing on all my vehicles.

There are probably more than 150,187 seminars you can take to learn how to care for your wealth. And another 34,876 schemes to help you become wealthy so you have something to care for. I don't have the secret to financial security. Frankly, some people just seem to make money, others seem to know how to give it and others still know how to use it with very little left over. Wealth is not democratically distributed and is not distributed in value-based criteria.

A good friend of mine, who has supported me and this ministry financially and prayerfully since the beginning, has often spoken of the joy he has in giving so that I can do what he could never do. And in that way he is sharing in the joy and fruit of my ministry along with others. I praise the Lord for the many people who give themselves daily to serve the Lord and others, so that they can obediently serve and support those areas that God is calling them to support, as their act of worship.

Wealth has many sides. We are sons and daughters of a King. We live as strangers in a world that does not acknowledge our Father, the King. Therefore, we are aliens, strangers in our land (1 Peter 2:11). We are worshippers in a context that disdains our God. We each contribute in some way to sharing the kingdom . . . . God does not use a cookie cutter. He gives principles. We seek his wisdom to see how those principles fit into our lives.

Giving is not about things or money. It's about walking a life of worship – where our worship impacts the way we live. Worshipping God means that we come to grips with the idea that the things of this world are not ours, but they are God's – we are simply caretakers of them for a time. Here are some things I try to do to practice the joy of giving:

1. Start like the Macedonians did; give yourself to God daily.

I frequently start my day by a simple prayer saying, "God, I am yours today. Use me in whatever way you need me." Look for ways that you can give. One day a young couple came to the doors of the church in which I worked. Often we re-direct these people to the food bank or social service agencies. But this day, I left my office and went shopping with them. I bought them groceries. They were unbelievably grateful. But I realized that their gratitude extended to much more than just the food I bought. They were shocked that I went with them, talked to them and prayed for them. Too often, in times of extreme need, they had been turned away.

2. Learn to serve others joyfully. Go with Nike and 'Just Do It'.

   Sometimes I think that service is really not about 'opening doors' and official roles. We make it much harder than it should be. Serving one another should be like breathing. We see a need that we can meet and we simply do it.

3. Tithe. A tithe is simply a portion of what you bring into your household. The Old Testament speaks of several tithes, the most common being a 10% tithe of your income.

   That's a good place to start. But don't let the percentage inhibit or prohibit you from responding to God in your giving. I encourage you to start with giving something on a regular basis and being willing to give extra when there is an extra need that God prompts you about. Tithing is a way of expressing your trust in God.

   As the Israelites wandered in the dessert, God literally sent food from heaven everyday. He told Moses to tell the people to gather just enough for that day. Because the Israelites were very human, after the first manna fell, many ran out into the fields and gathered much more than they needed for that day. Overnight, the extra manna rotted in their containers. God was livid – he wanted them to trust that the manna would fall again the next morning. That arrangement ended, but the model is true – God wants us to live in complete expectation that he will care for us tomorrow.

4. Give extravagantly above and beyond.

   There will always be needs within the church and community. Be willing to prayerfully consider where God might be asking you to give extra – a little or a lot – for the sake of his Kingdom's work. This is really about investment. Our Western culture has it a little confused. We see return on investment as cash – not lives. Think about your investment portfolio . . . . Where is your treasure?

5. Don't get caught in the misconception that giving means money. Sometimes, giving money is the easy way out. Giving means sharing what you have. That includes your time, your talent, your home, your possessions, your space.

There are times when I know giving money will be a quick fix. What God really needs me to do is to give my time. We are busy people. For some of us, our time is our most valuable resource. God is asking you to give – in creative and unexpected ways.

PART 3

Tying up the loose ends . . .

So, my dear brothers and sisters, be strong and steady,
always enthusiastic about the Lord's work,
for you know that nothing you do for the Lord is ever useless.
1 Corinthians 15:58 (NLT)

CHAPTER TWENTY-ONE

INSPIRING, ENTHUSIASTIC WORSHIP
Worship worth coming back for!

There are times when you experience God in a way that is momentous. For that moment, that fragment of time, you know you have come face-to-face with God in a way that jars your reality. And you know you can never be the same again.

If you have experienced it, you don't need to be told what it is. You can clearly remember the exhilaration that consumed your whole being with the sense that you were connected to the Lord of the Universe, the Ancient of Days. Given the opportunity to repeat that moment in time – you would gladly give up all else in order to return and experience that sense of consuming worship.

Sometimes inspiring worship happens at a conference. Sometimes at a retreat or camp meeting. Sometimes it happens in a small group setting. And sometimes it happens in a Sunday morning service. Sometimes it happens when you are all alone. But all you can know for sure is that you have been ruined for the ordinary. Anything less just doesn't satisfy.

Our penchant is to look simply on the outward characteristics of that moment. We might even believe that it is the concert itself that moved us – not the Holy Spirit's presence.

Throughout the church in North America people are trying to recreate an experience in worship that they had in a moment past. The link to 'true' worship has often come to be seen as a song, a worship style, a musical tradition. Just as the generation before us felt inspiration and a personal nearness to God in singing, *How Great Thou Art*, our generation has attributed style and form to a worship experience as well.

We go back to our congregations and push them to change the worship style in order to recreate that moment of inspirational experience. We begin to focus on changing our worship style partly because a different worship style has been a part of what brought about an encounter with God – an inspirational moment of worship for us.

Change often does that. We rearrange the furniture of our living room and our house feels newer, fresher, more inviting. My wife buys a new outfit or gets a new hairstyle and I notice her again for the first time – my interest and excitement is renewed. I get my hair permed and the house is once again filled with laughter (at my expense!). We buy a new or, at least, a newer car and driving is a fresh experience.

In our lives, in our relationships and sometimes even in our possessions, change helps to bring about renewed focus, renewed joy, exhilaration, anticipation and even revelation.

Changing how we worship God can sometimes do the same thing. We break out of that which is habitual to discover the wonder of a renewed love and devotion to the Lover of our souls. Once again, we begin to see his activity in our lives. We begin to listen more closely to the still, small voice of his Holy Spirit living within us. We become more concerned for the welfare and the salvation of our neighbours. All of this is good and all of this helps to make our worship inspiring, enthusiastic and that which people want to be a part of from week to week.

But we have to be very careful that we don't attribute the changing form of worship as *the way* to worship. Often what the change has really done is to awaken an awareness of God that incites our response to God.

Many studies on worship – worship styles, worship-wars, worship liturgy and what makes church worth coming back for – have been done among many churches of varying styles and demographics. What has been discovered, time and again, is that even though various church services may have different target audiences – Christians or non-Christian – their style may be liturgical or free, their language may be 'religious' or 'secular' – all in all, none of this really makes any overarching difference for church growth. Regardless of the variety of styles that these churches have, there are still many that are noted as having developed worship which is characterized by those who attend as 'inspiring' – not 'feel-good' inspiring, but rather a sense of the Holy Spirit being present. People attending these truly inspired services typically indicate that going to church is enjoyable – as opposed to a matter of fulfilling a duty.

We are creatures of habit who feel that if we can recreate an experience then we will attain inspiring, enthusiastic worship in our services. So we jump on the latest worship-style bandwagon and anticipate that our worship will be inspiring and enthusiastic. Ultimately, we try to renew our worship by programming inspirational worship rather than by living it.

Bruce Leafblad, professor of church music and worship at Southwestern Baptist Theological Seminary in Texas, writes:

> We should remember that renewal is not the same everywhere. In church history, no major renewal has ever come from forms and formats, and so it is today. The great need of the church today is neither to cling to the old nor to create new forms and formats. Our greatest need today is to recover the priority of God in our worship and in the whole of life. The crisis in worship today is not a crisis of form but of spirituality (Bruce Leafblad, 'Worship 101,' *Worship Leader Magazine,* November/December 1998, p. 25).

As professor Leafblad says, our crisis in worship today is not a crisis of form but of spirituality. We continually look outside for the change that needs to be taking place – inside! We continue to resurface and reface and rethink our forms and formats before considering the renovation of the spirit *by* the Spirit. Paul writes in 1 Thessalonians 5:16-19: "Be joyful always, pray continually; give thanks in all circumstances, for this is God's will for you in Christ Jesus. Do not put out the Spirit's fire."

And then Ephesians 5:15-20 he continues along this same theme, saying:

> So be careful how you live, not as fools but as those who are wise. Make the most of every opportunity for doing good in these evil days. Don't act thoughtlessly, but try to understand what the Lord wants you to do. Don't be drunk with wine, because that will ruin your life. Instead, let the Holy Spirit fill and control you. Then you will sing psalms and hymns and spiritual songs among yourselves, making music to the Lord in your hearts. And you will always give thanks for everything to God the Father in the name of our Lord Jesus Christ. (NLT)

When we feel disconnected from God, there is a greater likelihood that the problem is our hearts, not the format of the songs we are using. Are we joyful always? Do we pray continually? Do we give thanks in every situation? Do we take advantage of every opportunity to do good? Do we try to understand what the Lord wants us to do and do we continually ask the Holy Spirit to fill and control us?

Gaps in our honest and pure seeking of God's face, result in gaps in our worship experience and expression. Let's go back to that *How Great Thou Art* moment. Many people in the past generation sang the song in places like camp, where there was a heightened understanding of God's goodness and majesty as they sang around a campfire, beneath the shadowy trees, under the canopy of billions of stars. When the song is repeated, they feel that experience once again and renew the moment they felt in worship. While the emotions of worship are there, the experience can become less an intimacy with God and more of a memory.

Let's make it clear. Worship encompasses all of life – not just music. In corporate settings of worship, the experience you have has much more to do with the state of your heart and your own desire to see God face-to-face than with the skill of the worship team and service leader. Healthy corporate worship is dependent on the body of Christ interacting with God on a daily basis.

When we begin each Monday morning with a simple prayer saying, "Jesus, fill me with your Holy Spirit so that I might hear your voice today and understand what you are doing in me, through me and around me, as I go about my daily tasks," we open ourselves up to interact with God and have him interact with us. That's an act of worship – the beginning of a 'worship walk'.

And when our Monday ends with thanking God for the ways that he has made his presence known to us – even in the smallest of ways – we begin to open up our lives to be inspired and surprised by God. When our weeks are filled with those kinds of prayers and attitudes to have

God be an active part of our lives, our corporate gatherings to worship on Sunday mornings will take on a whole new life of inspirational, enthusiastic worship.

Jesus wants to interact with us throughout each day. He wants to draw us to worship him, praise him and thank him continually. The only way that happens is when we invite him to open our eyes and reveal himself to us and as we then keep an open eye, ear and heart for him to show himself to us.

When I teach at a variety of Discipleship Training Schools in Canada and the United States, I give the students an assignment. They are to come to class with an object of worship. The object they choose is one that reminds them of an attribute, characteristic, quality, or act of God. When they see it, they are reminded of who God is and what he is doing so they can respond to him in worship, praise, thanksgiving and rejoicing.

I am amazed at some of the things these young people have brought to class. One young man brought two rocks – one smooth, the other rough. He explained that he had found these two rocks about a meter apart alongside a river. Other than their outward texture they were much the same. One, he told us, was immersed in the running water while the other was on the river bank. This reminded him of two lives, both created in the likeness of God. One was immersed into the daily flow of the Holy Spirit; the other was only touched by the Spirit during an overwhelming flood. The analogy of the stones showed him that only when a person's life is immersed daily into the life of the Spirit do the rough edges of our humanity begin to wear away.

Great! He learned a wonderful lesson from those two unassuming stones!

Another girl brought a clump of burrs. For those unfamiliar with these weeds, a burr is a seed of a plant that has hooked barbs which grab and cling to socks, pants and the hair of animals passing by. It's one of God's creative ways of transplanting species. Being a city girl she had never seen a burr before. She was fascinated with them – nature's own Velcro! So she stuck them in her hair to hold it back – a primitive sort of barrette. Of course, this led to all sorts of interesting problems!

When she presented the burrs as an object of worship, she told the class that, although she hadn't originally thought of using these burrs as her objective article of worship, when she tried to remove the burrs from her hair she realized they demonstrated an attribute of God. God hangs on! He doesn't let go. It takes a concerted effort on your part to separate yourself from the burrs. But God never lets go!

Another young man brought a huge garbage container. He said the container reminded him that he can leave his garbage, the trash or sin that he struggles with, at God's feet. At his house the garbage gets taken out and hauled away every Thursday morning. But God 'cleans-up' his trash whenever he deposits it at his feet. When we confess our sins, our trash, our garbage, God removes it completely and forgets it was ever there (Hebrews 10:17)!

There have been many, many similar stories of young people finding things within their everyday experiences that direct their attention to a God who walks with them at all times and desires to commune with them every moment of every day. But perhaps the article of worship that has most impacted my daily 'seeing' God was the example contained in the Zip-Lock plastic bag.

During the class presentation, one student brought up what looked like an empty Zip-Lock bag. She began her description by saying: "Music doesn't do anything for me. It's not that I don't like music – I like it all right but it doesn't move me or impact me or make me think more or less about God. Music is just music. But I always feel near to God when it's windy. So I went outside and captured some wind in this Zip-Lock plastic bag.

When it's windy I love to go outside and walk in the wind. I love to sit at the base of a tree with my eyes shut, with the wind in my face and listen to the leaves clapping their praise to God."

Wow! What an awesome description of all creation giving praise to God, inviting us to join in.

Even today, every time I put leftovers into a Zip-Lock bag I think of the trees that clap their praise to God and I am drawn to worship him to whom the trees clap their praise. I even find that as I am shopping for groceries and walk down the plastic products aisle, my attention is drawn to God when I see the Zip-Lock section – and I worship!

> *You will live in joy and peace. The mountains and hills will burst into song, and the trees of the field will clap their hands! (Isaiah 55:12)*

So I encourage you to find signs in what you normally do every day that point to something that speaks of God, who he is, what he has done and is doing, and what he has said in his word.

If you are a truck driver – don't see your load as just another load – be reminded that God took the load we carry upon himself and hauls it away – and thank him for it.

If you are a mechanic don't see yourself as just replacing new parts for the old – be reminded that in Christ we are a new creation – the old things have passed away and all things have become new. And just like a mechanic, God is working to keep us functioning well, with periodic tune-ups.

If you are a teacher don't see your job as just trying to get across simple concepts to the children at your class – be reminded that Jesus gave us his Holy Spirit who would teach us all things and remind us of what Jesus has done – and praise his name.

I have a friend who is a carpenter – a very good one. When I would talk about being a worshipper of God each moment of everyday, he would often respond, "Gareth, that's easy for you to say. Worship is your job! Me? I'm a carpenter and I work with wood and dust and some pretty foul people sometimes. There's not a lot in each day to draw my attention to worshipping God."

I told him that he had perhaps one of the best occupations for being reminded – often – to worship God!

"Look at the wood you work with," I said as I swept away the dust and lightly dampened the wood grain, on a piece of oak wood he was working on, to make the grain stand out.

"Find two pieces of wood that have identical grain." It can't be done. Each tree is unique and each piece of wood from the trees is unique. Doesn't that say something about the incredible detail the God we serve has put into everything?

"What about the nails you use? Every time your hammer strikes a nail it can be a reminder of the One who took nails in his hands for you." For that matter, who was also a carpenter by trade? Jesus!

You see, we all have things that we do each day that can be used to help us 'see' God more clearly within the context of the ordinary. God wants to interact with us throughout each day of our lives. When we begin our days 'looking' for evidence and reminders of God we end our days having interacted with him in normal, healthy, life-giving ways.

Inspiring, enthusiastic worship has less to do with a place or a time or an event. It depends on our own daily preparation to be found as a worshipper of God at all times, in every situation and circumstance.

The Psalms encourage us to praise the Lord always with whatever we have – letting everything that has breath praise the Lord (Psalm 63:4; 104:33; 146:2; 150:6). We praise him with instruments and dancing. We praise him with our gifts and our talents. We praise him with our lives. And we praise him by testifying about what he has done and is doing in our lives; by telling others, our Christian and non-Christian friends, about how God has used us to do good in these evil days; about how he spared us from foolish things or about how he forgave us when we failed to be wise (Ephesians 5:15-20).

Inspiring worship happens best when we don't program it but when we begin to live it, to walk it out – inviting the Holy Spirit to fill and control us each day.

When you invite his filling and empowering in your life on a daily basis you will be amazed at how much he will reveal to you. And your response of worship will be contagious! There is nothing like a great testimony of God's intervention – even in the little things – to inspire worship in others. As that happens more and more, people will not want to miss what God is doing in his church. You will have inspiring, enthusiastic worship – not a program, but a living organism which will grow and produce fruit in your church and in the community.

Worship leader and music artist Kim Hill, in the book, *Experience God in Worship* says, "The style of our worship is not what is important, the motive and intent of our heart is. The extravagance of our worship is meant for an audience of One" (Kim Hill with Lisa Harper, Experience God in Worship; *Contemporary Worship: What Does Worship From the Heart Look Like?* [Loveland, CO: Group Publishing, 2000] p. 86).

To God be the Glory.

Here are some ideas that help me get started in being inspired to worship God each day.

1. Look for ordinary things that remind you of an attribute, characteristic, quality or act of God. Write it down. Meditate on it. How does it remind you to engage him in thought, in prayer and in worship?

   I find that often it is the repetitive things that we do each day that God can clearly speak through – if we only give him a chance. Use the little worship exercises at the ends of each chapter of this book in your small group or Bible class – you'll be surprised at what comes up. Ask a small child about worship and God – they have incredible insight.

2. Always be willing to respond to God in every circumstance. Again, this is where we need to be aware of the fact that God wants to communicate his presence to us at all times. Look for what he is doing around you and offer him your praise when you recognize it.

3. Read your Bible and ask God to give you understanding for what can apply to your daily living situations. When he draws your attention to something you've recognized of him – give him praise!

I've also concluded that whatever God does,
that's the way it's going to be, always.
No addition, no subtraction. God's done it and that's it.
That's so we'll quit asking questions and simply worship in holy fear.
Ecclesiastes 3:14 (Msg)

CHAPTER TWENTY-TWO

TO SUM IT UP
All good things come to an end

How do you really end a book on worship?

At some point you have to be willing to say, "Even though I've only scratched at the surface of seeing and understanding all the ways that God invites us to that place of a worship walk – living our worship – I need to stop."

If I were a movie maker, I would make plenty of room for a sequel.

Maybe there will be another book with more intersections between worship and living – a *Worship Walk 2,* perhaps? There are so many topics to cover! We have just grazed the surface. We haven't touched on worship and spiritual warfare, worship as intercession, worship and the manifest presence of God throughout the Bible, worship in different cultures and worshipping inter-culturally, worshipping through joy and laughter, things that hinder our worship and on and on . . . .

Over the years I have written and taught on many of these topics. I will continue to write *HeartCore – Make Us Holy*'s quarterly newsletter. Each issue deals with another aspect of the worship walk. I've received many phone calls, letters and emails encouraging me in what I was writing down and the inspiration it had given to lay people and leaders alike. Many of you encouraged me to collect these thoughts between the covers of a book. You are a big reason that this book has become a reality. The book has given me an opportunity to expand each topic.

This book is an exercise in faith – complete faith. I am not a writer. Facing the computer every day was not an easy task. More often than not, I quickly left the computer to fix something in the house. The house is in pretty good shape these days! We have painted the main floor, redone the kitchen and done a major re-wiring! It seemed that there was always something more pressing to do than to sit and write.

I love to discover new truths about God. I love talking to people. I even like teaching and preaching. But writing things down is a very solitary act and, for the most part, I am not a solitary person! Gayle says I write completely differently from how I interact with people. She says I try to sound academic and scholarly – but it doesn't work. So much for spousal encouragement!

But seriously, she is right!

But Gayle, and others, kept encouraging me along the way to the point of seeing this project completed. While running her own business along with her business partner, Kevin Hawley, keeping nine employees busy and paid, interacting with staff and clients – she has managed to squeeze in time to editing this book. She has taken my words and in editing them, made them sound more like I would have said them if I had been sitting across the table talking to you. So rest assured, all my comments about Gayle have been approved!

This project has been a collaboration of writing down my thoughts, inspirations and ideas, talking about them, discussing them and then Gayle helping to synthesize them into easily read and understood sections that carry the very essence of what I have written down and spoken about – but much more easily read!

Thank you, Gayle. I love you! *(How does one edit that? I am grateful to God for giving me a friend who has challenged me to walk in relationship with God in ways that have stretched my own imagination. I love you, too! [A note from Gayle: copy editor])*

So here I am – at the end of 10 years with *Make Us Holy* ministries – with at least a small portion of what God has spoken to me about a walk of worship everyday. I have only seen a fragment of what God is teaching me. I look forward to learning so much more. And God is still revealing all that he wants me to follow him in as I walk out this life of worship – loving, serving, listening, obeying and better understanding how much he values my relationship with him.

In 1989, God took me to Kitchener, Ontario, with a very clear call to "blow upon the coals and fan into flame the gifts of my people." I didn't realize at the time that the call included more than just what God wanted to do through me at the Kitchener Mennonite Brethren Church. But as I worked there for four and a half years as youth pastor, God began other stirrings in my being in regard to worship and walking out a life of worship. He began to open doors for me to minister with other churches and denominations. And he has been my guide and encourager along this road. He is the reason I am what I am today.

I encourage you to use these insights to prod you on to discovering more of what worshipping God – who walks with and among his creation – is all about. Look for more of what he wants to show you about his activity in and around you as you carry on ordinary tasks. Stretch the realm of interaction with God from the church to your life and living.

If this book has helped to open more doors of understanding for you about the multiplicity of ways in which God invites interaction with him, I would love to hear about it. Please feel free to give me a phone call or send an email.

Gareth J. Goossen
Office Phone: (519) 579-4321
Email: worshipwalk@makeusholy.org
Ministry Web Site: http://www.makeusholy.org
Book Web Site: http://www.makeusholy.org/worshipwalk

At all times, and indeed everywhere,
we acknowledge these things with the deepest gratitude.
Acts 24:3 (Phillips)

ACKNOWLEDGEMENTS

Many people have banded together to help me in starting and writing of this book. My thanks and praise go first to my Lord Jesus Christ who, by his Holy Spirit, continues to lead and guide me and show himself to me in many ways each day. He is the one who continues to teach me to 'worship walk'.

Secondly, my love and thanks go to my wife, Gayle, who, through her encouragement and her gifts of story telling, imagination and writing skill, has made this book a reality. She often talked through the components of these chapters with me, helping to point me in a direction and then coming alongside to edit what I wrote to better reflect what was in my heart. She worked countless hours editing, adding to and improving this book in addition to her already full schedule at work.

I also want to thank our three children (all of whom are now adults) for giving their dad up many, many times over the past ten years of this ministry. They sacrificed time with their dad so others could be encouraged in their walk of worship. I thank them for the ways that they encouraged me to keep writing by sometimes jokingly asking if I was just avoiding writing the book when they saw me fixing something in the house or starting a new project out in the garage. My prayer is that you would also learn to love to walk with Jesus in greater ways than I could ever have attained.

Thanks also go to my mom and dad, Helen & Jake Goossen (my dad passed away in 1998), who constantly loved and encouraged me. And even though they had no idea what this ministry I was wanting to start in 1994 was all about, they trusted in the One who had called me to do it – and they continually prayed and supported me in it.

Thank you, Lila Weber (Kitchener, ON), who has been my intercessor for the last ten years of ministry with *Make Us Holy* ministries. You have often spoken encouragement, and sometimes correction, to me when I needed it most. In spite of a lot of your own personal pain and trials you never stopped standing in the gap for me. Thank you!

Also, thank you to John Abbott (Dartmouth, NS) and Mardell Root (Manheim, PA) who have both given of themselves in intercession for me and this ministry, especially in the last few years. Again, your timely words of encouragement have often helped to bring clarity to vision and direction. John, your tenacity to 'speak from the hip' has often been just what was needed to help see clearly what God was doing and asking me to be involved in – through a 'preponderance of evidence.' Thanks, John, for the suggestion of the title, *Worship Walk.*

A hearty thank you to Susan Baker, my administrative assistant, who helped to look after a lot of the details of seeing this project come to completion. And to the *Make Us Holy* board of trustees – John Cassels, Rick DeVrye, Marie Fast, Robyn Serez, Ryan Snider – who believed in this project and have encouraged and supported me in the writing of this book over the last year and a half. Thanks also to past board members – Greg Clarke, Ed Heinrichs, Ron Lugowski, Connie Maier, Hazel Reimer, Ingrid VanVlymen, Arnie Wohlgemut, Paul Woodburn – who helped get this ministry off the ground and running, laying the foundation of what God has in store for the future.

Then, on the more practical side of things, thanks go to Gayle Goossen and Kevin Hawley who freely gave of the resources of Barefoot Creative – artists, designers, schedulers, editors, photographers – to help this book get off the computer and onto the printed page. Thanks especially to Heather Lee and Dan Snyder at Barefoot Creative who designed the cover, took the photo and designed the interior layout.

Thanks also to Marilyn Bender, Mark Bachmann, Alison Feuerwerker, Stephanie Donaldson, Kevin Boese (who also wrote a cover endorsement), Greg Reed and Hardy Schroeder who lent their hand and expertise in the proofing and final editing of this edition.

Many thanks to the many people who have helped, through their donations, to cover the costs of publishing this book. And others who have reviewed it and lent their comments for the cover and the forewords.

I am sure that I have missed some people along the way. It is not my intent. Rather, I am so very grateful for the many people who, over the years, have encouraged me through phone calls, emails or personal interactions to write these things down in book format. The fruit of those prayers, conversations and encouragements are what you now hold in your hands.

Walk with God. Worship him always.

To God be the Glory!

Every part of Scripture is God-breathed
and useful one way or another
— showing us truth, exposing our rebellion, correcting our mistakes,
training us to live God's way.
2 Timothy 3:16 (Msg)

BIBLE TRANSLATIONS USED

All Scripture references not otherwise noted are from the Holy Bible: New International Version. Copyright 1973, 1978, 1984 International Bible Society. Used by permission of Zondervan Publishing House.

NIV   ***The New International Version Bible***
Grand Rapids, MI: Zondervan Publishing House
International Bible Society; (1973, 1978, 1984)

NLT   ***The New Living Translation Bible***
Wheaton, IL: Tyndale House Publishers
(1996)

NCV   ***The New Century Version Bible***
Dallas, TX: Word Bibles
(1991)

Msg   ***The Message Bible***
Colorado Spring, CO: Navpress
(1993)

Phillips *New Testament in Modern English by J.B. Phillips*
New York, NY: Macmillan
(1958)

NAS *New American Standard Bible*
La Habra, CA: The lockman Foundation
(1960, 1962, 1963, 1968, 1971, 1972, 1973, 1975, 1977, 1995)

KJV *The King James Version Bible*
First set forth in 1611

BIBLIOGRAPHY

Bonhoeffer, Dietrich. *The Cost of Discipleship.* New York: Macmillan Publishing. 1963.

Carroll, Joseph. *How to Worship Jesus Christ.* Chicago: Moody Press. 1984.

Foxe, John. *Foxe's Book of Martyrs.* Online posting. The Third Persecution, Under Trajan, A.D. 108. 16 Oct. 2004. <http://www.connecticutadventist.org/Bible_Study/Foxe/Foxe_2.3.htm>.

Gustafson, Gerrit. "Worship Evangelism." *Charisma and Christian Life.* Oct 1991.

Hill, Kim with Lisa Harper. "Experience God in Worship"; *Contemporary Worship: What Does Worship From the Heart Look Like?* Loveland, CO: Group Publishing, 2000.

Jackman, Rev. John. *"Count Nicholas Ludwig von Zinzendorf."* Online posting. Zinzendorf: The Count Without Borders. 16 Oct. 2004. <http://www.zinzendorf.com/countz.htm>.

Leafblad, Bruce H. *"Worship 101,"* Worship Leader Magazine, November/December 1998.

Lightfoot, John. *"Exercitations upon the Evangelist St. John."* Online posting. A Commentary on the New Testament from the Talmud and Hebraic. 16 Oct. 2004. <http://www.ccel.org/pipeline/1-html/5-lightfoot-nt_talmud/john11.htm>.

Lloyd Jones, D. Martin. *The Presentation of the Gospel.* London: InterVarsity Press. 1949.

Martin, Paul. "When The Music Fades: The Eternal Truth Behind 'The Heart of Worship.'" Online posting. *Worship Leader Workshop Magazine.* 16 Oct. 2004. < http://www.worshipleaderworkshop.com/mag-when.htm>.

Rupert, Dennis. *"Eight Explanations for Suffering Found in the Bible."* Online posting. New Life Community Church. 16 Oct. 2004. <http://www.new-life.net/sufferng.htm>.

Tippit, Sammy. *"Prayer and Worship."* Online posting. Sammy Tippit Ministries: God's Love in Action. 16 Oct. 2004. <http://www.gospelcom.net/glia/2001/wow/st_043001.shtml>.

Tippit, Sammy. *"Suffering and Worship."* Online posting. Sammy Tippit Ministries: God's Love in Action. 16 Oct. 2004. <http://www.gospelcom.net/glia/2001/wow/st_032601.shtml>.

ABOUT THE AUTHOR

Gareth J. Goossen

Gareth Goossen is the executive director of *Make Us Holy* ministries. He has been instrumental in encouraging the church across denominations in North, Central and South America in their corporate worship and in their ability to enjoy the presence of God in everyday life. His passion is for renewal through worship, prayer and discipleship. Gareth is excited at the moving of God's Spirit, igniting the passion for God in young people and adults alike.

Gareth, together with his wife Gayle and family, followed God's call from their farm in Manitoba, Canada, to Fresno, CA, USA, where he attended the Mennonite Brethren Biblical Seminary, 1984–1986. Following graduation with a MA in New Testament Theology he pastored youth and young adults in two Canadian Mennonite Brethren Churches – Cariboo Bethel Church in Williams Lake, BC (1986–1989) and Kitchener Mennonite Brethren Church in Kitchener, ON (1989–1994). During this time God stirred Gareth's heart in worship and renewal. He has been actively leading worship for since 1986.

In 1993, Gareth organized the *Make Us Holy: Worship and Renewal Conference,* held at Waterloo Mennonite Brethren Church, Waterloo ON, Canada. It was here that he first met Peter Davids and Brian Doerksen. The conference was a watershed moment for the direction God was leading him.

As a result, in 1994 Gareth resigned as youth and worship pastor of Kitchener MB Church and began *Make Us Holy* ministries in response to the need for foundational teaching that invites renewal through worship, prayer and discipleship. Subsequently, Gareth taught several times at Brian's *Pacific Worship School* between 1994–1996 and led worship together with him at the *Winds of Renewal* Conference in Abbostford, BC, Novemeber 1994.

Gareth travels across North America and Latin America encouraging churches in their worship – many of who are going through transitions in their musical expression of worship. Gareth seeks to bring foundational teaching on worship to the church; create a middle ground of 'blessing' between the generations; work with worship teams to elevate expectation and excellence; and demonstrate passionate pursuit of Jesus in a daily walk of worship.

Gareth and his wife Gayle live in Kitchener, Ontario, Canada. They have three grown children. They are heavily involved in leadership responsibilities with their home church, *The Dwelling Place,* in Kitchener (<http://www.thedwellingplace.ca>). The focus of the church is to transform the community by becoming intimately involved in working and ministering within it. It desires to bring the presence of Jesus to the people in the community rather than to just invite the people in the community to the church – a church that is attempting to worship walk, intersecting the worship of the church with the life of the community!